CONCILIUM

CONCILIUM/VOL. 46

FUNDAMENTAL THEOLOGY

THE DEVELOPMENT
OF FUNDAMENTAL
THEOLOGY

edited by JOHANNES B. METZ

VOLUME 46

CONCILIUM
theology in the age of renewal

PAULIST PRESS
NEW YORK, N.Y./PARAMUS, N.J.

Library of Congress Catalogue Card Number: 74-92116

Suggested Decimal Classification: 211

Paulist Press assumes responsibility for the accuracy of the English trans-
lations in this Volume.

PAULIST PRESS
EXECUTIVE OFFICES: 304 W. 58th Street, New York, N.Y. and 404
   Sette Drive, Paramus, N.J.
Publisher: John A. Carr, C.S.P.

EDITORIAL OFFICES: 304 W. 58th Street, New York, N.Y.
Executive Editor: Kevin A. Lynch, C.S.P.
Managing Editor: Urban P. Intondi

Printed and bound in the United States of America by
Wickersham Printing Co., Lancaster, Pa.

CONTENTS

vii

PART II

BIBLIOGRAPHICAL SURVEY

PART III

DOCUMENTATION CONCILIUM
Office of the Executive Secretary
Nijmegen, Netherlands

PREFACE

Johannes B. Metz/*Münster, West Germany*
Werner Bröker/*Bonn, West Germany*
Willi Oelmuller/*Münster, West Germany*

I n this volume, which deals explicitly with fundamental theology, the purpose is to give the reader an insight into the general situation of fundamental theology rather than to deal with specific questions. We therefore have concentrated on underlying principles and examined attempts currently being made to put it on a new basis. Our starting point is the existing structure of various branches of theology—a structure that is now regarded as far less obvious and sacrosanct than in the past. And even if one takes the traditional divisions as a starting point, many questions remain about how to build up a fundamental theology that is relevant for today, for its own specific tasks make this branch of theology more deeply involved in constant change than others.

The first article gives a chronological view of the main tendencies and interpretations of fundamental theology in this century, examining their interconnnection and their increasing relevance for modern problems (Geffré). Allied with this is an article in the Bibliographical Survey dealing with apologetic tendencies in modern Protestant theology (Gilkey). Six authors from different countries or cultural regions single out what they consider to be the main points of organization, method and scope of a contemporary fundamental theology (Latourelle, Panikkar, Fries, Segundo, Walgrave, Cahill). These articles provide at least the beginning of proof that fundamental theology is more influenced by the contemporary situation than other branches of theology and that therefore any projected plan must reflect the historical, social and regional differences in the situation from which it starts. But at the same time these articles show various factors they have in common: a turning away from neo-Scholasticism and its thematic organization of fundamental theology, a change in aim and procedure, a new relationship to dogmatic theology and philosophy, etc. In this connection, see the article on "Apologetics" in *Sacramentum Mundi,* Vol. I, pp. 66-70.

One basic problem of fundamental theology—that of religious language—is dealt with in another article in the Bibliographical Survey in the light of modern linguistics (Macquarrie). Finally, there is an article on the increasingly urgent problem of how to present and justify the unity of faith in the growing pluralism of theological tendencies (Rahner).

PART I
ARTICLES

Claude Geffré, O.P./*Paris, France*

Recent Developments in Fundamental Theology: An Interpretation

I n contrast with the other theological disciplines, the nature of fundamental theology is still hotly debated among theologians.[1] The most common definitions today betray a definite uncertainty about the epistemology of a discipline which wants to fulfill at the same time the function of the old apologetics—i.e., that of providing a rational justification of the Christian faith—and exercise the critical function inherent in all science—i.e., that of explaining the basis and method of the science of theology.

Take, for example, the definition given in the recent French *Dictionary of Theology:* "Fundamental theology refers either to the defensive and justifying function of theology or to that sector of theology concerned with the study of the Word of God and man's acceptance of this Word." [2] According to Y. Congar, from whom this definition has been taken, one can consider funda-

[1] From a long list of studies, I specifically refer to the following: A. Gaboardi, "Teologia fondamentale. Il metodo apologetico," in *Problemi e Orientamenti di teologia dommatica* I (Milan, 1957), pp. 57-92; A. Lang, *Fundamentaltheologie. Die Sendung Christi* (Munich, [3]1962), pp. 8-40; G. Söhngen, "Fundamentaltheologie," in *Lex. Theol. u. Kirche* (4th ed.), pp. 452-59; A. Kolping, *Fundamentaltheologie* I (Münster, 1968), pp. 21-87; N. Dunas, "Les problèmes et le statut de l'Apologétique," in *Rev. Sc. Phil. et Théol.* 43 (1959), pp. 643-80; H. Bouillard, *Logique de la foi* (Paris, 1964), pp. 15-44.

[2] *Dictionnaire de la foi Chrétienne* I (Paris, 1968), col. 769.

5

mental theology as an integral part of theology (a treatise on the Word of God and its acceptance by man) or as a potential part (the defensive and justifying function).[3]

We might be tempted to see in this "justifying" function the most characteristic contribution of fundamental theology. While we would not want to return to the excesses that beset the apologetics of the old school, we should not reduce it either to a treatise on revelation or on the sources of theology (*loci theologici*).[4] It must always be concerned with showing forth the rational character of the act of faith. But we should add at once that Congar's definition does not explicitly mention a third function of fundamental theology—namely that of examining critically the nature and method of theology as a science, or in other words, providing theology with an epistemology and methodology.[5]

The meaning of fundamental theology is therefore somewhat variable, and this should make us beware of pinning it down to a too rigid definition as if it were once and for all perfectly clear about its object, its themes and its method. If its specific function is to explain Christianity to the human mind, one will already expect its set of subjects and even its method to develop according to the historical development of the mind. We shall thus have to allow even more room for historical relativity in the structure and practice of fundamental theology than in the other sectors of theology.

It is in this light that I would therefore like to try to interpret the recent history of fundamental theology. This is not going to

[3] Y. Congar, *La foi et la théologie* (Paris, 1962), p. 183.

[4] H. Bouillard suggests that we call the study of the *loci theologici* the "prolegomena to dogmatic theology" and that we reserve the expression "fundamental theology" for what is usually called "apologetics"; see his article "Human Experience as the Starting Point of Fundamental Theology," in *Concilium* 6 (1965), p. 80.

[5] Söhngen stresses this third meaning in his article referred to in footnote 1. See also the observations of J. P. Torrel, who compares this critical function of fundamental theology with the function of the treatise on criticism in philosophy, in "Chronique de théologie fondamentale," in *Rev. Thom.* 64 (1964), pp. 101-02.

be a historical sketch, however brief, of this theology from the beginning of this century.[6] But I believe that we can discern three main tendencies which followed each other chronologically, and this with a certain historical logic. We begin with the collapse of apologetics as an objective science to the benefit of a fundamental theology, the starting point of which is frankly theological and historical. From there we shall pass on to the *anthropocentric* view which inspires most modern works on fundamental theology. And this will lead us to the tendency which is beginning to take shape today and which reaches beyond objectivism and anthropocentrism to the social and political existence of modern man.

I

FROM APOLOGETICS TO FUNDAMENTAL THEOLOGY

Historical Background

The idea of an "apology of the faith" goes back to the origins of Christianity. One can find it already in the New Testament where its charter may be recognized in 1 Peter 3, 15: "Always have your answer ready for people who ask you the reason for the hope that you all have, but give it with courtesy and respect and with a clear conscience." But it was only in the context of the 18th century's interdenominational controversies that a science of apologetics was built up in order to create a methodical approach to this vindication of the Christian faith. Today the word "apologetics" has become suspect, and we may say that the era of "handbooks of apologetics" is now closed. The term is replaced by that of fundamental theology, a term already in use in the 19th century, in order to describe the discipline which aims at justifying the foundations of our faith and therefore of our theology.

Now, it is very instructive to look at the historical causes of

[6] For an historical outline, see A. Kolping, *op. cit.*, pp. 35-70.

this apologetic inflation in Catholic theology during the last centuries, and the reasons for its decline. This bent for apologetics can only be understood in connection with the Reformation, the rationalist triumph of the Enlightenment and the cultural phenomenon of atheism.[7]

Lutheran theology used to emphasize the subjective factors—particularly the part played by the Spirit—which give the certainty of the divine origin of our faith as soon as they make the believer accept the contents of revelation. Because of the reaction of the Counter-Reformation, Catholic theology insisted on the objective factors: that the object of the faith is presented by the Church as its norm (*ministra objecti*) and that it is possible to rationally prove the fact of revelation. In contrast with the patristic and medieval tradition which maintained that the light of faith makes us accept with certainty both the *fact* and the *contents* of revelation, Catholic theology began to yield to a very debatable distinction between the *contents* (the whole of unprovable truths) and the *fact* of revelation which, as such, could be proved. This tendency was encouraged by the controversies with the Rationalists and Deists of the Enlightenment who tried to reduce the truths of faith to truths that reason can comprehend.

At the very time that Catholic theology reacted against this dissolution of theology into philosophy by insisting on the obscure and unprovable character of strictly supernatural truths, it remained still imprisoned in this rationalism and tried to provide a rational proof of the fact of revelation at all costs. And so it developed a whole apologetic theology based on outward signs—the prophecies and especially the miracles—which were expected to provide the evidence for the fact that God revealed himself.

Apologetics as an Objective Science

And so in the 18th century we find manuals of apologetics which try to defend the truth of the Catholic religion against

---

[7] Cf. J. H. Walgrave, *Parole de Dieu et existence* (Paris, 1967), pp. 198-201, and also his article in this volume.

both the Rationalists and the Protestants by following a plan in three parts: (1) the existence of God and of religion (*demonstratio religiosa*); (2) the existence of the true religion (*demonstratio christiana*); the existence of the true Church (*demonstratio catholica*).[8] However, it is not until the beginning of the 20th century that we see the appearance of treatises in which the position of apologetics is explained with regard to both philosophy and dogmatic theology. In this field two works were outstanding: P. Gardeil's *La crédibilité et l'apologétique* (1908) and R. Garrigou-Lagrange's *De Revelatione* (1930).

The authors of these various projects had two things in common. First of all, they wanted to situate the science of apologetics within the faith, because apologetics cannot prove its own starting point, which is revelation, but only the credibility of this revelation. Second, because of their obsession with rationalism, they wanted at the same time to build up an objective science that could produce a maximum of evidence. According to Gardeil, "Apologetics is the science of the rational credibility of divine revelation." Its object is the credibility of Catholic dogma: "Credibility is the quality which Catholic dogma possesses because of the divine witness." For it is indeed "a property of revelation to be demonstrable by natural reason". By its formal object apologetics is therefore theological, while in its method it is a strictly rational and logical science. In the same way, Garrigou-Lagrange maintained that the proper function of apologetics is to present the revealed religion "in the light of the evidence for its credibility" (*sub ratione credibilitatis evidentiae*). It presupposes the faith but only appeals to rational arguments.[9]

[8] This threefold division appears already in P. Charron, *Des trois vérités* (1514), and in the Protestant thinker H. Grotius, *De veritate religionis christianae* (1627).

[9] I refer to the article "Apologétique" in *Dictionnaire d'Apologétique* where P. Le Bachelet defines apologetics as "the science whose object is to prove the fact of divine revelation considered as the foundation of the true religion or the science of the credibility of the Christian and Catholic religion" (I, col. 225). And the encyclical *Humani generis* declares that the outward signs dispensed by God "allow natural reason, even by itself, to prove the origin of the Christian religion with certainty".

The Failure of Apologetics as an Objective Science

During the last thirty years we have become far more aware of the grave limitations of the traditional apologetics of the text-books, particularly with regard to its concept of *revelation,* and this mainly through the renewal that took place in biblical studies. One may say that the *Constitution on Divine Revelation* of Vatican Council II has confirmed the progress which has taken place in fundamental theology during the last thirty years.[10] This no longer starts, as in the past, with an *a priori* concept of general revelation but, deliberately following the historical and theological method, proceeds straightaway from the concrete event of the revelation accomplished in Jesus Christ.

One of the great weaknesses of apologetics as an objective science lay in thinking that credibility was a characteristic that extended equally to all dogmas without having theologically and critically examined the key dogma of revelation itself. Revelation is a *transcendental* theological category in the sense that it precedes every single theological datum, while at the same time containing it.[11] That is why any fundamental theology which wants to be a critical justification of the *foundations* of theology must begin with a study of the notion of revelation. This revelation is not something that can be proved by sheer rational argument. It is the basic presupposition from which we start, and without which any truth that theology deals with collapses. We can therefore not proceed, as the old treatises on apologetics did, by asking ourselves the questions of the possibility, fittingness and need of revelation. We have to start straightaway with the event of revelation as recorded in Scripture and then try to disentangle its overall significance for the believer and for man in general in a given cultural situation.

Because of the *a priori* method used by the old apologetics,

[10] Cf. H. de Lubac, "Commentaire du préambule et du chapitre I," in *La Révélation divine* I (Paris, 1968), p. 283, who quotes P. Dejaifve, *Nouv. Rev. Théol.* (1966), p. 124.

[11] This expression is used by H. Fries, "Die Offenbarung," in *Mysterium Salutis* I (Einsiedeln, 1965), p. 159.

one can understand that the expression "apologetics" is being rejected more and more widely, and that the term "fundamental theology" is preferred as the science of the foundation of the faith (and hence of theology)—that is, the science of the dogma of revelation itself. "Thus setting up the apology of this dogma, and hence demonstrating its credibility, we will then *ipso facto* ensure the credibility of all other dogmas which spring from it; it will provide the faith with a foundation and theology with its principles." [12]

Another shortcoming of apologetics as an objective science, and the direct result of its abstract notion of revelation, is that it takes as obvious the distinction between "what God reveals" and the fact "that God reveals". This view leads to a dangerously extrinsic distinction between the judgment of credibility of the fact of revelation and the assent in faith to the contents of that revelation. It presupposes an intellectual notion of revelation as a "communication of truths that cannot be proved" and it forgets that it is the very fact of revelation which is the object of the Good News of the Gospel. Some authors might be tempted, under the influence of Bultmann, to say that the order is wrong, because one could say that all men can already have a certain preliminary understanding of the content of revelation as the message of salvation but that the unforeseeable and unprovable character of the Good News lies in the fact that this salvation is already in fact given to us in Jesus Christ.[18]

As long as the wholly abstract notion prevailed of a revelation conceived as communication of supernatural truths, it was possible to pretend that one could demonstrate the evidence of the credibility of the fact of revelation (i.e., such a revelation is neither physically nor morally contrary to God or man) without

[12] N. Dunas, "Les problèmes et le statut de l'apologétique," in *Rev. sc. phil. théol.* 43 (1959), p. 679. Even if it does not convey the whole program of a fundamental theology, many authors would accept the following definition: "A critical theology of the Word of God in its being and its manifestations, in its sources and its means of expression" (*ibid.*, p. 680).

[13] See L. Bakker, "What Is Man's Place in Divine Revelation?" in *Concilium,* 21 (1967), p. 31.

bothering about the content. When we return to the biblical—that is, the historical, personalist and christocentric—notion of revelation as put forth in the *Constitution on Divine Revelation,* we can see that the exact dividing line between fundamental and dogmatic theology is difficult to trace. Fundamental theology also takes into account matter belonging to other dogmatic treatises. But we still have to ask ourselves how fundamental theology specifically looks at the mysteries of faith.

Finally we must mention the most serious deficiency of apologetics as an objective science, and the major reason why it is criticized by modern apologists. The objection is that the old apologetics proceeded with a *rational credibility* which nowhere joined up with the *lived credibility of the believer.* Hence the deceptive character of those scientific manuals of apologetics which try to provide decisive arguments of a metaphysical, physical and historical nature to prove the truth of the Christian religion and the Catholic Church, and which have never convinced anyone yet. Today we are more aware of the mistake of using an apologetic method derived from the religious controversies of the past and collecting external motives of credibility to explain how and why a definite concrete person should accept the faith.

Here we see how strongly the method and favorite themes of any fundamental theology are influenced by the social and cultural context. One can only court failure by trying to apply today a method of apologetics which flourished in the cultural climate of the Enlightenment. As J. Walgrave put it: "For the modern man, deductive reason is no longer a 'separate mental faculty' (*intellectus separatus*) which defines the truth of life by its own light, in order to apply it afterward to practical conduct. It has become increasingly evident that thought at large—and thought about the truths of life particularly—cannot hover somewhere above or outside life, but that it can only move within conscious life itself, taken as a whole." [14]

In other words, when we are dealing with a value like religion,

[14] J. H. Walgrave, *op. cit.,* p. 202.

the judgment of credibility cannot be limited to mere reason. It depends on a free and existential option, or at least on some basic ethical judgment. At the present time, therefore, while the rational justification of the faith remains a valid pursuit, such a justification will no longer limit itself to extrinsic proofs for the divine origin of Christianity, but will rather start with an explanation of what it means to live the faith today within the Church and within this world. To vindicate the faith is a matter of showing the meaning of Christianity for the conscience of someone who is already involved morally in an historical situation.

The Human Credibility of Christianity

These grave defects of objective, too purely intellectual and too extrinsic apologetics explain the success of the what has been called "the apologetics of immanence" (cf. Blondel's *L'Action*, 1893) and Rousselot's view.[15] The merit of the so-called *subjective* apologetics was that it showed up the formal credibility of the other type, based only on rational argument and ignoring such affective elements as the "intention of belief", regarding them as but a skeleton, a mere abstraction.

During the last thirty years, however, an attempt has been made to overcome the false dilemma between an objective and a subjective apologetics. Authors use the term *integral apologetics* to describe a kind of apologetics which tries to maintain the value of the affective factors that are implied in real credibility. This does not mean that it has become a theology of conversion or "the art" of apologetics, but rather that it tries to analyze the objective structures of the subjective faith. And here Blondel's analysis of the internal logic of human action has proved most fruitful. In this way, the object of such an apologetic approach is no longer merely the rational credibility, but the *human credibil-*

[15] While traditional apologetics admitted that the judgment of credibility preceded the act of faith and made it reasonable, Rousselot thought that this judgment did not precede but was implied in the act of faith: the light of faith lets us see that credibility. Rousselot's view was developed by Tiberghien and de Masure.

ity of Christianity.[16] And we have at last clearly realized that it is simply not enough to try to vindicate the truth of Christianity by starting from historical proofs.

In conclusion, then, one can understand why the term "fundamental theology" is now preferred to describe Christian apologetics. It is not simply that in an age of dialogue the word "apologetics" is discredited. It is rather, and more profoundly, that we have become conscious of the weakness of apologetics when it pretends to be able to prove the *fact* of revelation on historical grounds. We can only be sure of divine revelation within the experience of faith. From the start, fundamental theology insists on its theological and historical character. It proceeds to a *critical* examination of the twofold foundation of Christian existence—namely revelation and faith. And within this critical process it exercises its function of *justifying* the validity of both. It bases the rational character of the act of faith on the way Christianity corresponds to the existence of man in all its dimensions.[17] I would like for a moment to concentrate on this major preoccupation of fundamental theology by stressing its *anthropocentric* approach.

II

THE ANTHROPOCENTRIC APPROACH OF FUNDAMENTAL THEOLOGY

When we try to explain the development that has taken place in fundamental theology during the last thirty years, we realize that it fits in with the urge to overcome the intellectualist and objectivist way in which neo-Thomism saw the problems. We can

[16] The expression "the *human* credibility of Christianity" appears in P. A. Liege, "Bulletin d'Apologétique," in *Rev. sc. phil. théol.* 33 (1949), p. 67.

[17] H. Bouillard, "Human Experience as the Starting Point of Fundamental Theology," in *Concilium* 6 (1965), pp. 79f. His plan for apologetics must be understood in this perspective. Taking up Blondel's "immanent" approach, he tries to show that our relation to the Absolute is and must be with reference to the dynamism of our will, in order to bring out the fact that Christianity is the historical determination of this relation.

no longer rest content with the analysis of a purely rational credibility because this no longer corresponds to our modern frame of mind. If fundamental theology aims at "justifying" the faith in the eyes of both the believer and the unbeliever, it has to take into account the philosophical and cultural situation which conditions our mind. Therefore, the best students of fundamental theology will take note of the changes that have affected human understanding since Kant; they will take man's historicity much more seriously, and they will not overlook the fact that today we have reached the age of criticism, or, rather, of hermeneutics. This is the background to that "anthropocentric" concern which is evident in so much work in fundamental theology today.

The Functional Orientation of Theology

One might define the program of fundamental theology by saying that it must deal with the *anthropocentric dimension of the whole of theology*. This consideration of the human viewpoint is something generally required for all dogmatic theology, but it is the specific function of fundamental theology to provide a critical vindication of dogmatic theology from the angle of a transcendental analysis of man.

Traditional theology, which found its highest expression in Thomas Aquinas, represents an admirable attempt to understand the eternal content of the mystery of God and the mysteries of faith. Modern theology is more concerned with bringing out the *meaning* of the Christian mystery as a whole for people today. It therefore wants to be more existential, more anthropocentric. This tendency, moreover corresponds to the development of theological thought about revelation, of which I have already spoken. Biblical revelation only speaks to us of God as he is in himself insofar as it is implied in his action *for us;* it is always a dispensation and functional—that is, "saving". On the other hand, one cannot separate thinking about the fulfillment of revelation in history from thinking about its fulfillment in the believer. In contrast with the extrinsic explanations of revelation as a communication of supernatural truths addressed to the human sub-

ject as a passive receptacle, we must say that the meaningful
activity of God's people becomes a constitutive element in revelation itself. We may therefore say that revelation is already a
tradition and even hermeneutical.

Finally, modern theology attempts to draw the consequences
of Bultmann's basic intuition about the necessary preunder-
standing which is involved whenever we try to read again the
Christian message. It wants to provide all at once and inseparably an interpretation of the Word of God and of man's existence. There is no revelation in the full sense if the gift of God's
original Word does not coincide with a revelation of man to himself. As Paul Ricoeur put it: "Revelation as such is an opening
up of existence, a possibility of existing." [18] The understanding
of Christianity can therefore not be severed from reflection upon
man as a mysterious opening up, a looking for meaning and
direction.

A number of authors therefore seek to develop a dialectic of
man's existence where Christianity can be seen as giving meaning and fulfillment to mankind. I have already alluded to H.
Bouillard's plan for an apologetic which, following Blondel,
starts from the will as passing from the phase of striving to that
of full determination, and tries to show that the Christian faith
is the necessary, though inaccessible, condition of man's destiny.
But I would like to refer especially to Karl Rahner's ideas about
the necessary relation between theology and transcendental
anthropology.

The Anthropocentric Approach and the
Transcendental Problem

"Transcendental" here means the *a priori* condition for the life
of the spirit, that which makes it possible for anything to become
the object of thought, will or love. For Rahner, God is the *a
priori* condition of all our spiritual activity. To adopt a transcendental reference (*problématique*) or to treat the whole of dogma

[18] P. Ricoeur, "Le langage de la foi," in *Bulletin du Centre protestant
d'Etudes* 16 (June, 1964), p. 31.

as transcendental anthropology means "to investigate, in regard
to any topic of dogma, the conditions of its knowledge in the
subject—here, in the theologian; it will show that there are
indeed *a priori* conditions for the knowledge of this topic, and
that these conditions already imply something of this topic or
object, and of the way, the method and the limits of its being
known".[19]

To apply a transcendental method to theology means, finally,
to show the link between dogmatic statements and human experience as the object of reflection. Revelation is always concerned
with man's salvation. Now, only too often dogmatic statements of
the Christian faith appear esoteric or mythical because they show
no connection with man's experience in his effort to understand
himself. It is therefore up to the theologian to bring out the
anthropocentric dimension of the statements of faith—that is, to
show the link between what these statements envisage and
man's self-understanding. I would say that this is the special
function of the fundamental theologian because, by laying bare
this anthropocentric dimension of all theology, he shows at the
same time that the mysteries of the Christian faith are credible.

Karl Rahner does not, of course, deny the radically "theocen-
tric" character of Christian theology insofar as its content is concerned. But he thinks that if we take the anthropological orientation of modern philosophy seriously, we must try to show the
meaning of revelation as intelligible for our contemporaries on
the basis of a profoundly "anthropocentric" understanding.

Clearly, the danger of such an approach is that it might take
the meaning out of the gratuitousness of revelation as the history
of salvation and that "one might deduce by some strict and necessary logic all the theological propositions from this single experience of oneself as the source of their objectivity and their conceptual articulation".[20] Rahner explicitly rejects this new kind
of modernism. But the whole problem of a fundamental theology

[19] K. Rahner, "Theology and Anthropology," in *The Word in History*
(New York, 1968).
[20] *Ibid.*

which thus makes use of the transcendental method is the delicate articulation of the relation between man's existence as the transcendental *a priori* condition of the faith and Christianity as the *a posteriori* historical condition. In fact, Rahner can only avoid the danger of a necessary deduction by using an anthropology which already owes much to the light of revelation. His concept of theology as transcendental anthropolgy is unintelligible if one does not know his bold thesis about the relation between grace and nature. One can show a link between the structures of human existence and the content of dogmatic statements by pointing to the fact that " 'nature', understood as spiritual, personal and transcendental, is an intrinsic, constitutive and necessary element, not of grace as such, seen in the abstract, but of the reality and the event in which grace can be effectively given".[21]

Therefore, one cannot reproach Rahner with starting from an anthropology which would owe nothing to revelation and which would reduce this revelation to its own measure,[22] but one could object that his idea of the autonomy of philosophy is debatable. However, here we get involved in the permanent controversy about the relation between philosophy of religion and fundamental theology. In any case, Blondel has proved that it is possible to respect the autonomy of philosophy without depriving oneself of the new philosophical contribution brought about by revelation.

Fundamental and Dogmatic Theology

At present it is more important to stress that this transcendental character of fundamental theology forces us to reassess the relation between fundamental theology and dogmatic theology. If many people today doubt the *fact* of divine revelation, the reason is that they have difficulties with the *content* of revelation. It would therefore seem that the critical and justifying function of

[21] *Ibid.*
[22] This is the only point on which I disagree with L. Malevez in his finely balanced article on the twofold tendency in contemporary theology, "Présence de la théologie à Dieu et à l'homme," in *Nouv. Rev. Théol.* 90 (1968), p. 799.

fundamental theology must operate in every dogmatic treatise. As Rahner suggests, we should have a far greater interpenetration of fundamental theology and dogma than we have at present.[23] Without denying that the proper function of special dogmatic theology is to arrive at an understanding of the content of each mystery of faith, it would appear true to say that the more theology becomes a hermeneutical science, the more the distinction between fundamental theology and dogmatic theology will tend to get submerged.

Whereas Rahner speaks about the "anthropocentrism" of theology, one might just as well speak about its need to be hermeneutical, in the very broad sense that we cannot assert anything about God which does not imply some assertion about man. In other words, we need a theological knowledge concerned not only with knowing the objective truth of dogmatic statements but also with their meaning for man today. When we understand the hermeneutical function of theology, we are simply following up the implications of Heidegger's hermeneutical phenomenology when he says that all knowledge of being can only be arrived at in the light of that particular being which examines being—namely, man.[24]

We should be able to maintain this hermeneutical requirement without slipping into the extremes of an impenitent Bultmannism which runs the risk of reducing theology to mere anthropology. I can only interpret history through the living interpretation of myself as an historical being constantly tending toward self-fulfillment. As Schillebeeckx said: "Understanding the faith and self-interpretation cannot be separated."[25]

---

[23] K. Rahner, *op. cit.* See also his "Ueber die theoretische Ausbildung künftiger priester heute," in *Schriften zur Theologie* VI (Einsiedeln, 1965), p. 154.

[24] On Heidegger's hermeneutical phenomenology, based on the hermeneutics of factual reality, see O. Pöggeler, *Der Denkweg Martin Heideggers* (Pfullingen, 1963), pp. 70f.

[25] "Revelation presupposes man's quest for himself as the condition for the meaning of his self. That is why faith, the confession of faith and dogma can only have meaning *in* man's self-understanding. . . . Man's self-understanding is therefore an internal dimension of revelation it-

Today, therefore, we would define fundamental theology as the *critical* and *hermeneutical* function of all theology. It is "critical" in the sense that it analyzes the condition of historical possibility and the transcendental condition of the faith: on the one hand, the event of revelation, and, on the other, man's existence as the *a priori* condition of the faith. Its proper and complex function is to let the *a priori* condition and the historical *a posteriori* condition of the faith illuminate each other. It is "hermeneutical" in the sense that it tries to disentangle the lasting significance of the statements of faith in their scriptural, dogmatic and theological form through man's understanding of himself and of his relation to the world.

On the basis of what has been said, we might divide the course in fundamental theology into two major sections: the study of the fulfillment of revelation in history, and the fulfillment of revelation in the believing subject. But we should stress that this is a formal distinction, since revelation necessarily implies human subjectivity where it is fulfilled in faith, and one cannot study the faith without considering its relation to the historical event of revelation.

We see, then, that while it is true that this critical and hermeneutical function is required today for all theology, it finds a particularly explicit expression in the two major sections of any fundamental theology: revelation and faith.

III
FUNDAMENTAL THEOLOGY MUST LOOK TO THE FUTURE

I have tried to bring out the anthropocentric orientation of modern fundamental theology. This orientation must be interpreted as a sign of the historical situation with which faith is presented in this world. Many people accept Christianity in general while feeling ill at ease with this or that particular statement of

---

self": E. Schillebeeckx, "The Understanding of Faith and Self-Interpretation," in *The Word in History* (New York, 1968).

the Christian faith. It would be precisely the task of this new kind of fundamental theology, advocated by Rahner, to provide a "vindication of the faith, lived before it is thought".[26] We should put together what, at the existential prescientific level, would *justify* the belief of an educated man today (because faith must be "reasonable").[27]

Yet, it seems clear from the more recent and significant studies in this field that authors have already begun to see the limitations and dangers of this inflation of anthropology. There is a fear that we may make man the measure of the Word of God. It is also said against the use of the transcendental dimension that it puts transcendental subjectivity before man as an historical and political being, and that it therefore overcomes idealism only in appearance.

Man as the Measure of Revelation

One could level the same reproach at both the anthropological intent of fundamental theology and Bultmann's existential hermeneutics. Under the pretext that the language of revelation has become unintelligible for many people today, it has been so carefully adapted to their understanding that the very content of the message is in danger of losing all meaning. God has been reduced to the meaning he may have for man as he understands himself and his relation to others, and so man has become the measure of revelation.

In one of the most important contributions to today's fundamental theology, Hans Urs von Balthasar has sounded a serious warning against the dangers of anthropocentrism in theology. Without quoting Rahner directly, he sees in the use of the immanent or transcendental method the danger of "a hidden and sometimes explicit philosophizing where the internal measure of the seeking spirit—seen as empty, or simply vacant, or as the 'restless heart', or as a *potentia obedientialis* (a natural tendency to seek God), etc.—is somehow turned into the measure of

---

[26] K. Rahner, "Ueber die theoretische Ausbildung künftiger Priester heute," in *Schriften zur Theologie VI* (Einsiedeln, 1965), p. 152.
[27] *Ibid.*

revelation".[28] He thinks that this kind of tendency finds its
extreme expression in modernism "where the objective facts of
revelation become totally dependent on the subjective internal
and dynamic relationship of revelation between God and the
soul, and are only valid for the Christian insofar as they
effectively support and foster this dynamic relationship".[29]

In contrast with this, von Balthasar approaches the question
from a contemplative angle, and tries to show the splendor of the
figure of Christ (he calls it the aesthetic aspect of revelation) as
the manifestation and celebration of absolute love—that is, the
love which reigns within the Trinity and God's love for mankind: "Only love is worthy of belief." Christ is the concrete form
of absolute love; he finds his vindication in himself, whatever the
subjective condition of man: "The figure we meet in history is
convincing in itself because the light in which it manifests itself
radiates of its own strength and clearly proves itself in its own
radiation." [30]

Basically, von Balthasar reminds the theologians that instead
of trying to explain the newness of revelation on the basis of
some previous condition which falls back ultimately on human
reason, they should let the revelation manifest its meaning on the
basis of its concrete origin, the figure of the Word incarnate. One
might be inclined to say that von Balthasar has taken Heidegger's warning very seriously: "As long as the building of
anthropological and sociological as well as existentialist concepts
has not been overcome and abandoned, theology will never
acquire the freedom to express what it has been entrusted
with." [31]

This is not the place to join in the controversy about a pluralistic theology within Christianity. Following Malevez, I would

[28] H. Urs von Balthasar, *Herrlichkeit* I (Einsiedeln, 1961), p. 142,
quoted by L. Malevez, *art. cit.*, p. 794.

[29] *Ibid.*

[30] *Ibid.*, p. 446.

[31] Quoted by H. Ott, "Was ist systematische Theologie?" in *Der spätere
Heidegger und die Theologie* (Zurich, 1964), p. 132.

simply point out that von Balthasar himself cannot wholly do without some kind of pre-understanding. I can only apprehend the beauty of the mystery of Christ if I already have within me some kind of norm of beauty, and it is because I perceive there a certain affinity that I can come to credibility.[32] It is the function of the fundamental theologian to analyze and organize this pre-comprehension. On the other hand, even in Bultmann the historical *a posteriori* of the revelation as the event of grace can never be deduced from the comprehension of man. Revelation is defined precisely by the fact that it is beyond the power of man. Finally, I repeat that we should not forget that the transcendental anthropology from which theologians like Rahner start to show the credibility of Christianity already owes a great deal to the light of revelation.

An Excessively Individualistic Concept of Man

The transcendental approach is not only attacked by those who maintain that it reduces the mystery content of revelation too much to man's measure. Others object that it is too bound up with individualistic categories and with faith in the *present* phase as an existential encounter between God and man. A purely transcendental, personalist and existential theology becomes inadequate as soon as in this age of "secularization" the new understanding of the world requires a more penetrating reflection on the relations between the Christian faith and the world. In particular, it is unable to treat the world as *history* with the seriousness it demands. The most lucid protagonists of this new tendency are the Protestant J. Moltmann and the Catholic J. B. Metz.[33] They would prefer to say that the main theme of fundamental theology is no longer the relation between theory and practice. They want it to concentrate on the social and political

---

[32] L. Malevez, *art. cit.,* p. 797.

[33] See esp. J. Moltmann, *Theologie der Hoffnung* (Munich, 1965) and J. B. Metz, "L'Eglise et le monde," in *Théologie d'aujourd'hui et de demain* (Paris, 1967), pp. 139-54 and "The Church's Social Function in the Light of a 'Political Theology'," in *Concilium* 36 (1968), pp. 2-18.

implications of the Christian faith. This is why fundamental theology will increasingly become the platform for the dialogue between faith and the human sciences, and not only between faith and philosophy as in the past.

Fundamental Theology as "Political Theology"

According to these authors, in the post-religious situation of our time, when the world is no longer an object of contemplation but an immense workshop and man is defined by his boundless capacity to build a world that is always new, it is the proper function of fundamental theology to spell out the "dimension of the future" and the social-political orientation of Christianity. It should particularly show the biblical foundation (the Old Testament is about the "promise") of this orientation toward the future which characterizes our modern culture and toward an understanding of the world as history which results from it.

In other words, it is the dimension of the *future* which enables our thought to reach beyond the limitations of an anthropocentric theology too exclusively concerned with the value of the decision of faith for the present moment. With this dimension of the future, one can interpret "the world as history, history as the history of the end, faith as hope and theology as eschatology".[34] For J. B. Metz it is not enough that fundamental theology introduces the anthropocentric dimension into the whole of theology; our present spiritual situation urgently requires that we lay bare the "eschatological dimension" of all theology: "Eschatology is not just one discipline side by side with other disciplines. It is the fundamental dimension which determines, and shapes, every theological development, particularly with regard to the world. The attempt to interpret the whole of theology on an existential or personalist basis is an important contribution to theology. . . . But this existential and 'anthropocentric' theology can easily remain foreign to the world and to history if eschatology is not brought in as an essential element. Only in the eschatological perspective of hope can the world appear as history. Only when

[34] J. B. Metz, "L'Eglise et le monde," *op. cit.*, p. 140.

we understand the world as history can our free action be given its rightful place: in the center." [35]

The world is nothing but an immense field of potentiality waiting for the free creativity of man striving toward the future with his whole being. In this age of secularization the only theology that can account for both the Christian hope and the hope of this earth simultaneously is neither a theology of the cosmos nor a transcendental theology of man's existence, but a *political theology*—i.e., a theology which takes the social and political dimension of man seriously, in the way man understands himself today. According to J. B. Metz, the function of such a theology is twofold. On the one hand, it will critically examine the individualistic tendency still current among contemporary theologians. No doubt, the private sector and the ineffable encounter between God and individual man constitute the specific territory of existential hermeneutics and a kind of theological personalism. On the other hand, "the positive function of political theology tries to determine a new kind of relationship between religion and society, between the Church and the social reality of public life, between an eschatological faith and the practical reality of society".[36]

Fundamental Theology and the Border Problems between Church and World

This new "political" trend in fundamental theology shows how much its problems are conditioned by the situation of the faith in this world. No doubt, the traditional themes of fundamental theology (the historical and rational foundations of Christianity and the critical explanation of the essence, method and language of theology) require more penetrating research and will always do so. But if the primary task of fundamental theology is to justify Christian hope in a given historical situation, it is there that we must sort out the relations between the Church and the world on

[35] *Ibid.*, pp. 147-48.
[36] J. B. Metz, "The Church's Social Function in the Light of a 'Political Theology'," *op. cit.*, p. 6.

the lines of the *Pastoral Constitution on the Church in the Modern World*. The theologian must not only bear witness to the permanent aspects of the Word of God, but he must also deal with the new human issues in their relation to the content of revelation. He must begin by *sharing* in man's understanding of himself, his world and his future, so that he can judge the great issues which beset the Christian conscience with a genuine critical understanding in the light of the faith. As Schillebeeckx said: "To ask about the inspiration of the Gospel as detached from the concrete content of our own existential experience is to ask a question without substance, and to this one can only give an unrelated and existentially meaningless answer." [37] However, all too often both believers and nonbelievers have the impression that the Christian Churches continue to confess a doctrine that is admirable but irrelevant to man's most urgent problems. It is not good enough to claim an admirable nature for Christianity and then to ignore the failures of Christianity in history. The critical and liberating force of the Gospel must be manifested in thought and action. The answer of the Gospel will always be paradoxical. It disputes man's self-sufficiency, and it doubts excessively optimistic ideologies about man's future. But at the same time, precisely in virtue of its eschatological dimension, it sets man free and urges him on in his earthly expectations: the humanization of man, the socialization of mankind, and the building of an order of universal peace and justice.

I cannot list here all the border problems with which a modern fundamental theology should concern itself. But one may confidently assert that they will primarily concern the relations between faith and the new forms of atheism (the theology of unbelief), the Christian interpretation of ideological and religious pluralism (theology of non-Christian religions), the confrontation between faith and the political and social reality (theology of violence), and the reinterpretation of Christian life in

[37] E. Schillebeeckx, "La théologie du renouveau parle de Dieu," in *La théologie du renouveau* I (Montreal/Paris, 1968), p. 102.

the context of a secularized world (theology of the realities of this world).

In conclusion, it seems right to say that the most active research in fundamental theology is trying to reach beyond the objectivism of neo-Scholastic theology as well as the anthropocentrism of existential theology. We are witnessing the birth of a new kind of fundamental theology which intends to embody man's new self-understanding, particularly his understanding of the future on this earth. As in the past it tries to make Christianity credible, but by stressing its social and eschatological dimension. And only those who have forgotten the unique destiny of the Church and the world in God's plan will be astonished to see fundamental theology so ardently pursue extra-theological problems.

René Latourelle, S.J./*Rome, Italy*

Dismemberment or Renewal of Fundamental Theology?

I

THE SEARCH FOR A CENTER OF UNITY

The assertion has been made many times concerning preconciliar fundamental theology that it was searching for its identity: its object, method, structure and limits.[1] In the aftermath of Vatican Council II when ecclesiastical studies are being restructured in three cycles, the crisis—far from being resolved—seems to be aggravated. In the first cycle, since the time allotted to the presentation of the whole of the Christian mystery is more and more reduced, there is a great temptation to sacrifice a discipline which is already so imperiled. Key experiments, in Europe or in America, demonstrate that fundamental theology has no other alternative at the present time than to dismember itself and disappear or to begin a new life.

In certain places, fundamental theology no longer exists as such. One part has been turned over to christology (divinity of Christ), another to exegesis (problem of the gospels), and the rest to the philosophy of religion and to the history of religions. Elsewhere, it has been absorbed by dogma: it no longer exists as the special province of theological studies, with its own themes

[1] R. Latourelle, "Apologétique et Fondamentale. Problèmes de nature et de méthode," in *Salesianum* 28 (1965), pp. 256-73; A. Kolping, "Fundamentaltheologie im heutigen Hochschulunterricht," in *Theologie u. Glaube* 54 (1954), pp. 115-26.

and problems. It is coextensive with dogma, as one of its dimensions: it surfaces on *occasion,* when theological reflection would seem to require it. Elsewhere, religious verification or the problem of Christianity is identified with the global presentation of the Christian kerygma. Emphasis is placed on the fact that the kerygma has a *meaning,* in itself and for man, which renders it acceptable to man. What it is especially interested in is the Christ of faith.

Where fundamental theology subsists as such, its place and importance vary from one country to another. Some place it at the beginning of theological studies; others position it at the end of theology, as a critical reflection concerning the totality of the object of faith already known and catalogued; still others suggest a global presentation, at the beginning of theology, of the theme of revelation and faith, with an in-depth treatment of certain questions at the end of theology. The emphases especially vary from one country to another.

In some countries attention is centered on the importance of historical and exegetical questions: to show that Christianity is really rooted in history. In this view, emphasis is placed on the history of salvation, on the manifestation, witness, and signs of Christ, on the value of the gospels as historical documents, and on the problems of hermeneutics and demythologization. Others stress the question of the *meaning* of revelation and mystery for man. This accounts for the importance of philosophical approaches in the spirit of M. Blondel, K. Rahner and H. Bouillard. Still others pass rapidly over the problems of historical criticism and resolutely undertake a theology of revelation, the faith and the Church.

In this perspective of a fundamental theology asking questions about itself (reason for being and center of unity), we will briefly indicate what we believe to be the object, the method, the constants and the variables, as well as the most pressing tasks of present-day fundamental theology. We will then conclude with suggestions of a pedagogical order.

II
THEOLOGY OF THE WORD OF GOD AND THE FAITH

If we ask what is the pole of attraction and center of unity of seemingly heterogeneous questions which are the concern of fundamental theology, we believe that this center is the *Word of God* and the reality which it confronts: *the faith of man.*

Fundamental theology is designated as such above all because it studies the *first* reality of Christianity—that is, the revelation of the Word of God to mankind.

This reality, which constitutes the privileged object of fundamental theology, presents a twofold aspect: it is at once both an *event* of history, identifiable in time, and a *mystery* of faith. It is the primordial mystery, bearer of all the others as well as the first and decisive event of Christianity. Revelation even owes one part of its richness to this twofold aspect of mystery and event. It follows that fundamental theology, in order to be faithful to its object, must apply itself to the understanding of the Word of God, but in its *totality*—that is, in its mysterious being, in its historical unraveling, in the signs of this unraveling, in the objective forms by which it expresses itself and perdures throughout the centuries (tradition and Scripture), and in its authentic interpreter (the magisterium).

Moreover, this is the mode of procedure of the *Constitution on Divine Revelation* which might well become the charter of fundamental theology. The Constitution sets forth first the mystery of revelation (nature, object, finality); then it deals with revelation in its historical development (preparation in the Old Testament, fulfillment in Jesus Christ) and in man's faith or response. It next treats of the transmission of revelation through tradition and the inspired scriptures, both interpreted by the magisterium which is simultaneously an auditor and a servant of the Word. Revelation and faith (event and mystery), transmission (tradition and Scripture), and interpretation of revelation (magisterium): it is always a question of one and the same object.

Thus rooted in the Word of God and man's response, fundamental theology with one and the same stroke formulates the *first categories* of theology. Revelation and faith, tradition and inspiration, dogmas and magisterium are analogous, in theology, to the notions of being, truth, certitude, evidence and objectivity in philosophy. Hence, it pertains to the first understanding of the faith to explore and define these basic notions implicated in the whole theological development.

In this perspective of a fundamental theology with the binomial Word-Faith as its center of unification and unity, dogmatic treatment and apologetic treatment—far from being in opposition—complete and stimulate one another with respect to a better understanding of the object studied. Why, then, separate the event from the mystery by an arbitrary and dangerous vivisection when one contains the other? Fundamental theology will speak dogmatically concerning mystery and apologetically concerning event. If it diversifies its approach, it is out of fidelity to the real.[2]

III

CONSTANTS AND VARIABLES OF FUNDAMENTAL THEOLOGY

The binomial Word-Faith, with its related themes, constitutes what some might call the *constants* of fundamental theology. Theology could never dispense with reflecting on these themes, for they are, as it were, the framework of Christianity. Side by side with these constants of fundamental theology are found the factors of *variability* which are related to its very condition as a discipline of frontiers, and oblige it to make continual adjustments.

[2] R. Latourelle, *Théologie, science du salut* (Bruges-Paris-Montreal, 1968), pp. 101-05; *Théologie de la Révélation* (Bruges-Paris, [3]1969).

Some of these variables which nowadays affect fundamental theology are:

1. *The category of history.* Contemporary man has become aware of the essential historicity of his condition. Theology itself, without minimizing the *nature* of mysteries, forcefully stresses the historical character of revelation and salvation. It is founded on the history of salvation and on *salvation-in-history*. The God of revelation is a God who *intervenes* by a series of events culminating in the event *par excellence* which is Christ.

2. *Anthropocentrism and personalism.* Contemporary thought is formulated in an anthropocentric type of structure. Man is no longer merely one object among others; he has become the center of everything, the universal point of reference. Medieval theocentrism has given way to anthropocentrism. Consequently, fundamental theology desires to be not only the understanding of the Word of God but also the understanding of the *meaning* which the intervention of God in man's history by means of the flesh and language of man can have for man. It investigates the meaning that a Christic religion can have for man.

3. *Social or "political" dimension.* For a long time theology reduced faith to a choice of a strictly private character. As a result, the adventure of salvation, including the final vision, unfolded in the strict intimacy of two partners: God and myself. Contemporary theology has rediscovered the social or "political" character of Christianity.[3] It is the task of fundamental theology to improve this essential dimension of revelation, faith and salvation.

4. *Global perspective.* As is the case with the other theological disciplines, fundamental theology is cultivated out of a desire for unification and unity. It is concerned with understanding the *whole* of reality. Hence, instead of opposing a revelation-event to a revelation-doctrine, a revelation-encounter to a revelation-truth, it strives to show rather that revelation, in accord with the

[3] J. B. Metz, "The Church's Social Function in the Light of a 'Political Theology'," in *Concilium* 36 (1968), pp. 2-18.

viewpoint under consideration, is at once divine action, historical event and history, witness and message, encounter and communion. In the case of faith, it emphasizes not merely the character of assent to the revealed message but also the character of total giving (intelligence and will) to the God who reveals and gives himself.[4]

5. *Ecumenical dimension.* Under the influence of the present ecumenical climate, fundamental theology is elaborated in a spirit of dialogue. The dialogue between theologians is extended and carried on with other Christian communities, with the great religions of the world, and even with contemporary atheism. This attitude of acceptance rests on the recognition of the truth-content of other systems of thought and belief. One of the most intense forms of present-day dialogue is the dialogue that has been begun with the philosophy of our time.

6. *At the service of the believer.* In a world where all the spiritual families and all forms of belief and unbelief exist side by side, the unbeliever's questions touch the very heart of the believer. The latter feels the need, more than ever, to justify in his own eyes his existence as a believer. It must be candidly admitted that the most acute problems of the present Christian consciousness have to do with *God-in-Jesus Christ:* these are problems of fundamental theology. Hence, fundamental theology must be first of all at the service of the believer.[5]

---

[4] J. Alfaro, S.J., "The Dual Aspect of Faith: Entrusting Oneself to God and Acceptance of the Christian Message," in *Concilium* 21 (1967), pp. 53-66; R. Latourelle, *Théologie, science du salut, op. cit.,* pp. 245-47.

[5] J. B. Metz, "Apologetik," in *Sacramentum Mundi* I, pp. 66-70; "Unbelief as a Theological Problem," in *Concilium* 6 (1965), pp. 59-77.

IV
URGENT TASKS OF FUNDAMENTAL THEOLOGY TODAY

At the present time there are three problems which seem particularly pressing to us: the problem of the historical dimension of revelation, the problem of religious verification or the problem of signs, and the hermeneutic problem. But actually, it is always a question of one and the same problem—that is, the intervention of God in the world of man: in time, in the flesh, and in language.

Christianity and Temporality

The problem of the relations between Christianity and history poses a whole series of problems which succeed one another in fits and starts. A first group of problems concerns the very history of salvation. If salvation is the history of the free and loving self-communication of God to man of all times, what is the relation of this (fundamental, universal) transcendental revelation to the Judaeo-Christian revelation? In other words, if millennia separate Adam from Moses and the prophets, did the men of this pre-Christian age have the benefit of revelation and faith? On the other hand, if God's self-communication to historical and social man tends to be objectified and explicitated in rites, doctrines and practices, what do non-Christian religions represent in the economy of revelation and the faith? Are they not valid and desired expressions of the fundamental revelation made to mankind? [6]

Judaeo-Christian revelation also poses problems of its own. In Israel, the infinite is revealed in figures of a temporal and finite existence. It takes shape in a people which receives revela-

[6] A. Darlap, "Fundamentaltheologie der Heilsgeschichte," in *Mysterium salutis* I (Einsiedeln-Zürich-Köln, 1965), pp. 3-153; G. Thils, *Propos et problèmes de la théologie des religions non-chrétiennes* (Paris, 1966).

tion in its history and reproduces it in the categories of a particular age and in specific institutions: royalty, the temple, Jerusalem. How can a revelation which is at this point tied in with the categories of a particular age and the doings of a single people escape the vicissitudes of history? [7] Above all, how can it claim to have value for men of all ages?

We know that history is an interpersonal event which introduces us to the heart of persons; it is a witness. This is especially true of the apostolic witness. The apostles and evangelists tell us of the shock produced on them by their encounter with the God-Man. We find ourselves confronted with an historical witness which is inseparably a witness of faith: event and salvific value. Consequently, in those confessions of faith which the gospels constitute, is it possible to rediscover the authentic figure of Jesus of Nazareth and to hear his message? Has not the interpretation of the apostles, and later that of the Church, deformed, exaggerated, or at the very least transfigured the nature of the facts and their meaning? How can the primitive kerygma be rediscovered under the layers superimposed by the apostolic preaching, ecclesial preaching and the redaction of the evangelists?

The Hermeneutic Problem

We see then that the problem of the relation between Christianity and history leads us to pose the hermeneutic problem—that is, the problem of the relation of Scripture to the word and the word to the event. Indeed, the confrontation of Scripture with the critical, philological and historical sciences has made us more conscious than formerly of the problems of interpretation. The hermeneutic problem can be elucidated only if it is dealt with on all its levels. [8]

First of all, there is a history of the hermeneutic problem. This history has experienced three principal phases. A first phase, at

[7] R. Latourelle, *Théologie de la Révélation, op. cit.,* pp. 417-34.

[8] R. Marlé, *Introduction to Hermeneutics* (London and New York, 1967); P. Ricoeur, Preface to R. Bultmann, *Jésus: Mythologie et démythologisation* (Paris, 1968), pp. 9-28.

the beginning of Christianity, was consecrated to the deciphering of the Old Testament with the aid of the New Testament. The second phase, which coincided with the Middle Ages and the theory of the four senses of Scripture, was an attempt to interpret human existence, in particular the moral life, and the whole of human reality, in the light of Scripture. The third phase began with the relatively recent discovery that the New Testament is not only interpretative with respect to the Old Testament but it must itself be interpreted in its literal sense.

As we have seen, this necessity of an interpretation is inherent to the witness-character of the kerygma; it also indicates the slight though real gulf which exists between an event on the one hand (life and words of Christ) and its preaching and consignment to writing on the other. To decipher the New Testament entails interpreting the witness of the primitive Church concerning Jesus of Nazareth; it entails discovering the relation between the object of faith and the profession of faith.

Associated with this third phase of the history of Christian hermeneutic is the problem of *demythologizing*, since this enterprise is born of a desire for a better understanding of the text which expresses the event. In this practice of demythologizing as originally set forth and realized by Bultmann, it is important to distinguish demythologization as a work of science, as a work of philosophy and as a work of faith; it is also important to stress how these three forms and levels can clash and lead to aberrant conclusions. If it is perfectly legitimate, for example, to eliminate a pre-scientific and outdated conception of the world from the Bible, it is unacceptable to eliminate—in the name of the outmoded philosophy of the 19th century—every intervention of God in human history under the form of miracle, resurrection, and incarnation. These clashes lead not only to demythologization but also to univocal and solitary dialogue of man with man.

Finally, reflection on the hermeneutic problem should be extended as far as considerations on the phenomenology of language and the ontology of speech. In this regard, structuralism by casting grave suspicion on human language has brought into question the validity of religious language itself.[9] Is the latter capable of expressing faith in a truly significant word? By incarnating itself in the language of a particular age, is not the Word of God a prisoner of the restraining forces which language (system and structures) exercises on man? If language is incapable of expressing the *subject* speaking, how can God himself make use of it to express his own mystery? Present discussions on structuralism have already elicited useful reflections for a theology of revelation. They have shown, for example, how *language* (system and structures) and *word* (act of the subject and creativity) are connected in the labor of speech, and how the subject strips away anonymity from language. They have also stressed the whole importance of symbolic language as the privileged expression of the mystery of the person.[10]

Religious Verification or the Problem of Signs

A third urgent problem of contemporary fundamental theology is once again a problem of interpretation and meaning: it is the problem of identification of Christ as the Son of God through the signs of his glory. As a result of the decline of apologetics, the theology of signs has for several decades been relegated to the second level of theological reflection to the great harm of the faith itself; for the problem of religious verification is inescapable: faith is man's entire remittance to God, but it is not retreat into unconsciousness.

Since Christ is the human, corporal form through which God encounters man and manifests himself to him, the salvific pres-

[9] On this subject, see *Esprit* (May 1967 and November 1963). Cf. especially P. Ricoeur, "La structure, le mot et l'événement," in *Esprit* (May, 1967), pp. 801-21; J.-P. De Rudder, "Structural Elements in the Word of Revelation," in *Concilium* 36 (1968), pp. 63-71; F. Tricaud, "Vérité, langage, tradition, structure," in *Lumière et Vie* 88 (1968), pp. 9-26; F.-M. Genuyt, "Peut-on parler de Dieu?" in *Lumière et Vie* 88 (1968), pp. 42-77.

[10] A. Dulles, "Myth, Symbol and the Biblical Revelation," in *Revelation and the Quest for Unity* (Washington, 1968), pp. 20-46.

ence of God in the world is properly verifiable only through the mediation of the man Jesus. Hence, he is the enigma, the mystery, that must be unraveled. The question of the Jews remains our own: "What sign do you show us?" (Jn. 2, 18; 6, 30). Otherwise, there is no other recourse but fideism. Theology then comes down to the study of signs, but this time with a sharper critical sense, one that is better equipped on the exegetical and historical level, more conscious of the complexity of the problems it encounters and, consequently, less categoric in its affirmations.

The study of the signs of revelation is itself also affected by the hermeneutic problem. What characterizes it, however, is the concern to relate the signs to Christ and his person. The signs which enable Christ to be identified are not external to Christ: they are Christ himself, living and complete, in the multiform radiance of his manifestation to the world.

A theology of signs must take account of the resistance of contemporary man. What bothers contemporary man is the sort of *unintelligibility* that signs (notably, miracle and resurrection) introduce into a world which possesses its own intelligibility. Hence, it would seem urgent to demonstrate how the economy of signs is connected with the economy of salvation. If it is apparent that the signs of revelation are not elements of incoherence in an order which has its own consistency, but the organic elements of an *economy* marvelously adapted both to a revelation which comes to us through the ways of history and the flesh, and to the profound nature of man to whom it is addressed, and if it is apparent that this economy is no less marvelous than the one which unites the mysteries among themselves, man will undoubtedly show himself to be less rebellious to the idea of an intervention of God in the cosmos and in history.

Up to the present, the theology of signs, influenced by Vatican Council I and by anti-rationalist apologetics, has favored miracles and prophecies-predictions. A theology of signs that wishes to be authentic and complete must be rooted above all in the fundamental signs of Christianity—that is, Christ, the Church and the message of salvation itself. Vatican Council II—by a process of personalization and interiorization characteristic of the entire work of the Council—has given value to the witness of a holy life. And this is truly just, for since the Gospel is promulgated and the Spirit is given so that we might live from the Word, the great sign of salvation is life in and with the Gospel—that is, the transformation of man into a new creature, vivified by the Spirit, and the transformation of mankind gathered together in unity and love.[11] Hence, there is reason for giving value also to the sign of the Church by a methodic reflection on the actions of the Spirit in the history and life of the Church.

V

PEDAGOGICAL ASPECTS

After these reflections on the major theme, method, principles of inspiration, and urgent tasks of fundamental theology today, we wish to make some remarks of a pedagogical nature.

In the first cycle (basic course), if we wish to take account of the extremely mottled preparation of students and their level of maturity, on the one hand, and the nature of the problems treated, on the other, it appears that fundamental theology should be situated at the two ends of theology. It is desirable to distinguish a first series of problems which must be dealt with by the beginners in theology (revelation and signs, tradition and inspiration, dogma and magisterium, faith and theology), and another series of problems which are no less essential but more conveniently presented at the end of theology (or even in the second cycle), either by reason of their intrinsic difficulties, or

[11] R. Latourelle, "Le Christ, Signe de la Révélation selon la Constitution Dei Verbum," in *Gregorianum* 47 (1966), pp. 685-709; "L'économie des signes de la Révélation," in *Sciences Ecclésiastiques* 19 (1967), pp. 7-31; "Vatican II et les signes de la Révélation," in *Gregorianum* 49 (1968), pp. 225-52; "La sainteté, signe de la Révélation," in *Gregorianum* 46 (1956), pp. 36-65.

again because they presuppose a view of the whole of theology in order to be dealt with correctly.

Thus rooted in the Word of God and on the faith of man, primary and basic realities of Christianity, but at the same time sensitive to the currents of thought of contemporary man, fundamental theology—far from dissolving and disappearing—could experience a new springtime while waiting until new signs of the times oblige it to rethink and redefine itself.

Raymond Panikkar/*Varanasi, India*

Metatheology or Diacritical Theology as Fundamental Theology

A Parable

A teacher who was a Westerner or trained along Western lines was almost in despair, for after a carefully built-up scientific explanation of malaria—its process, causes, etc.—the boys of the Uganda primary school did not seem to have understood anything. "Why does a man catch malaria?" asked a boy timidly. "Because a mosquito, the carrier of the parasite, bites him," replied the teacher, who went on to give the whole explanation again. At this the class, still unconvinced, and solidly behind the daring boy, shouted, "But who sent the mosquito to bite the man?" For those Uganda boys, the schoolmaster had neither understood nor explained anything. They were not concerned with facts, scientific "hows" or efficient causes, but with the living world (and the final cause perhaps), with the existentially relevant issue—for the real thing about malaria (imagine you or one of your family having it) is why that particular individual has been bitten by that particular mosquito. Fundamental theology is like that teacher, and two-thirds or perhaps even three-fourths of our present day generation resemble the Uganda school boys. Unless I can explain why the mosquito has bitten me . . .

The Two Meanings of Fundamental Theology

Fundamental theology, as commonly understood, is a pre-theological or philosophical reflection on the foundations of the-

43

ology. This reflection is directed either to justifying the assertions of Christian doctrine—which discipline is traditionally called "apologetics"—or to finding out the very sources and foundations of theology. The former proposes to be a rational or at least reasonable justification of the elements elaborated by theology; the latter claims to be a disclosure of the very basis of theological self-understanding. It is to the second aspect that I shall restrict myself.

Assumptions and Presuppositions

A group of *assumptions* and another of *presuppositions* underlie this—by now traditional—fundamental theology. Some of the *assumptions* are based on the concept that theology needs a foundation that is in some fashion outside it; others are founded on the idea that the basis can be known.

These assumptions were at the very starting point of the discipline even before it received its present name. One could discuss what these grounds are and the extent of the difficulty in knowing them; however, Christian theologians, by and large, as soon as the discipline acquired consistency (that is, as soon as they felt the need of a foundation for theology *outside* theology), took it for granted that such was the correct way of stating the problem. One of the most striking examples of this mode of thought was Vatican Council I, so many of whose pronouncements have a fundamental-theological orientation.

Central to this manner of thinking is a dualistic conception of reality: God and the world, increate and created, the ground and the erection above it. In this two-story building of nature and supernature, grace is based on nature, faith on reason, theology on philosophy and the like. To be sure, the foundations are called *preambula* and not *fundamenta*—in order to maintain the freedom and "gratuity" of the upper story—but they amount to the same thing. If, for instance, you do not admit that there is a God and a soul, how can Christian teaching make sense to you?

Some of the *presuppositions* are based on the idea that the above foundations are human and universal, or, in other words, valid for all human beings without distinction. In consequence, a certain degree of "civilization" was believed to be necessary for one to adhere to the message of the Church. In addition, methods like the so-called pre-catechetical instruction or *évangélisation de base*—a certain philosophical indoctrination of the concepts of "person", "nature", "substance" and "individual" and "private property", the preaching of monogamy, the effort to convince people of the preferability of other manners in eating and dress, etc.—were considered as parts of the Christian kerygma, necessary pre-conditions to the proclaiming of the Gospel.

The Crisis of the Presuppositions

The distinction between presuppositions and assumptions seems to me to be of capital importance. An *assumption* is something which I assume for many possible reasons—traditional, heuristic, axiomatic, pragmatic, hypothetical, etc. It is a principle which I set at the basis of a thinking process in a more or less explicit way. A *presupposition,* on the other hand, is something which I uncritically and unreflectively take for granted. It belongs to the myth from which I proceed and out of which I draw the raw material to feed my thought. The moment a presupposition is known to be the basis of thought or the starting point of a process, it ceases to be a *pre*-supposition. Only another person—or I myself in a second moment—can make me aware of my presuppositions; when that happens, I cannot hold them as I had done previously, but am led to either reject them, or to keep them as "suppositions" or as assumptions. This is also why, at the moment theology becomes more aware of its presuppositions either through criticism from the outside or through acquiring a critical perspective, theologians begin to question the until then unquestioned basis of their science. The crisis thus produced is of the sort that any living reality must experience in its growth.

Now, theology and fundamental theology were at home in one particular culture and world view: what they took for granted were the presuppositions of the Western world. The two sciences were grounded on the same myth and shared many common pre-suppositions—some of which have been laid bare in the present day encounter of mentalities, with the consequent confusion in the theological field.

Indeed, these uncovered presuppositions have also been questioned as assumptions. The present generation finds the traditional scheme insufficient. In fact, the ground on which theology rests today has become more problematic than the Christian content itself.

The Challenge of Universality

The real challenge to Christian faith today comes from within —i.e., from its own exigency of universality, from its own claim of having a truly "catholic" character. Any message directed to the whole of mankind today which takes a part for the whole, or which ignores the variety of peoples, cultures and religions, is bound to be discarded at the very outset. The Christian faith will either accept this challenge or declare its particular allegiance to a single culture and thus renounce its claim of being the carrier of a universally acceptable message, which does not destroy any positive value.

The problem of fundamental theology today cannot be solved merely by extrapolating, without a previous justification, a set of propositions which may be meaningful within a certain cultural or religious context, but which are irrelevant, meaningless or even unacceptable outside it. If fundamental theology is to have any relevance at all in our time of world communication, it has to make sense to those outside the cultural area of the Western world and, incidentally, also to those within it who no longer think, imagine and act according to the paradigms of traditional fundamental theology. A simple glance at the history of the world will convince us that the differences between cultures are not minor and that what we conceive as an incontrovertible principle may not be so in another culture. The world at large today is no longer prone to commit the mistake of imagining that everybody thinks and feels alike simply because the outer manifestations of behavior are similar. The encounter of peoples, cultures and religions is a major problem for fundamental theology, a problem which indeed challenges its very anthropological and philosophical foundations. It is in this connection that I would like to put forward some general considerations.

Foundations, A Priori and A Posteriori

The problem, serious and central as it is, cannot be ignored or explained away, assuming that others will sooner or later understand or be converted to our point of view. Those times are over. Our problem is that of searching for the foundations of Christian theology on a basis which at least makes sense for peoples living beyond the cultural area out of which fundamental theology has traditionally grown.

The only possible method for finding the foundations of theology has to be *a posteriori*. In other words, fundamental theology is not at the beginning of the theological reflection, but at its end. It is not that the Christian faith is based on those foundations, but rather that the effort at understanding a Christian fact leads us to discover some of the conditions of its intelligibility under some given circumstances.

History is also here a wise master. All sorts of ideas that not too long ago were considered fundamental to Christian theology are dismissed today as accidental, because other possible interpretations, which may eventually be more plausible, have been found—interpretations which claim to save the real message precisely by purifying it from its adherence to obsolete world views.

The real difficulty lies in finding the criterion for this operation. How am I to know whether something is essential to my faith or not? Where will the end of the operation be, once I begin demythologizing?

The Unity between Theology and Fundamental Theology

The thesis I am proposing tries to reestablish the unity—and, by this, the harmony—between theology and fundamental theology. It considers the latter neither a necessary epistemological condition for the former, nor its ontological basis. If theology would depend on the acceptance of an extra-theological basis, it would then lose not only all its wisdom character but also all its intellectual cogency; it would become utterly at the mercy of that philosophy which would offer a better backing to the theological thesis. Theology would then be totally dependent on the auction of the philosophical (or not even philosophical) market place.

What I am proposing is the recovery of fundamental theology as a fundamentally theological endeavor—i.e., as fundamentally theology. The very fact of reincorporating fundamental theology into theology will explode the far too narrow cage in which theology has been sometimes confined; it will liberate theology from the tutelage of philosophy, making it no longer dependent on one particular philosophy or world view outside itself.

Accordingly, fundamental theology is considered to be that theological activity (for which so often there is no room in certain theologies) which critically examines its assumptions and is always ready to question its own presuppositions. However, it does so not as a separated platform on which in a second moment faith builds up another construction of its own, but rather as that effort at intelligibility of the actual theological situation in any given context. There is a difference, indeed, between the content of the Christian faith and the conditions of its intelligibility, but it is not a real distinction, for the content of my faith is nothing but an intelligible crystallization of faith itself. Content means intelligible content. And a content is not such if it rests on explicitly non-understood premises.

I am saying that the anthropological conditions necessary to the understanding and acceptance of the Christian message cannot and are not to be severed from the interpretations of its content. Let me elaborate this point by means of an example.

The Buddhist, the Hindu and the Secularist

The existence of God has been traditionally considered a philosophical truth independent of any theology, so that it is supposed to be one of the foundations of Christian doctrine; the resurrection of Christ, on the other hand, would belong to the purely theological order. It is usually said that if you do not accept the existence of God, you cannot understand what the Christian faith is all about; it is also generally affirmed that if you do not accept the resurrection of Christ, you cannot be called a Christian. The difference between those statements is that whereas to admit the existence of God you do not need the specifically Christian faith, you do in order to accept the resurrection of Christ; therefore, the affirmation "Christ is risen" could be taken to be the shortest and most accurate expression of the Christian faith.

Now, the situation today is more complex. Let us abruptly confront our above example with a triple fact: that of a Buddhist not believing in a God of whatever type and yet having a highly developed and refined religion; that of a Hindu having no objection whatsoever to the resurrection of Christ; and that of a secularist theologian or modern Western man affirming himself to be a Christian and yet accepting neither God nor the resurrection as they are traditionally understood.

The Buddhist would like to believe in the whole message of Christ, and he sincerely thinks that he could accept it and even understand it better if it could be purified from what he considers to be its theistic superstructure. The Hindu will wonder why he has to join a physical and cultural community simply because of his belief in the divinity of Christ and in his resurrection. The "death of God" theologian, or whatever name we may choose for him, will say that it is precisely because Christ is the Savior that he can dispense with any conception of a transcendent God or a physical miracle.

The answer to the question as to whether these three persons can be called Christians will depend on the interpretation of what they say—i.e., on what they really *mean* to say. I shall not enter here into the merits of the above arguments. All I choose to say is that the three statements offer the same pattern and that it would be artificial and not conducive to clarification to lodge the former into fundamental theology, or the second into theology, or the third into philosophy. All depends on what we understand by God and how we picture Christ's resurrection, on our assumptions and their context, and how the Christian faith can be maintained within such different religious, epistemological and metaphysical patterns. For instance, is it necessary to have a theistic and substantivized conception of the divinity to be loyal to the Christian faith? Does one need to have a literal and fundamentalistic picture of the resurrection to be an orthodox believer? Is it essential to hold the Aristotelian-Thomist philosophical scheme to meaningfully accept the Christian message? Do I really have to admit some *preambula fidei* as part of faith itself, or does it all depend on the interpretation I give to what faith tells me, so that the same faith may have different *preambula?*

The Catholic existential answer is very clear to the individual: your interpretation—that is, your understanding of the Christian fact—must be personally intelligible, but it has to be also in harmony with tradition and thus with the magisterium, because dogma is also an historical reality. However, we are not dealing now with a problem of discipline or with an individual case. My question would be whether tradition and the magisterium have the right to prevent the entry into the Church to those whose lives are guided by different patterns of intelligibility—or, stating the same problem more properly, whether the present-day historical crystallization of the Christian faith is the only possible one. The Church has theoretically never said this, though the difficulty lies in discovering whether and which formulations are equivalent. The problem remains whether or not and up to what extent the several patterns can sustain and convey the Christian *kerygma.* And here only history will have the last word. The Church herself is inscribed in the historical process.

The Function of Fundamental Theology

To become aware of the problem is already to be on the way to overcome it. The weird fact, however, is that this awareness is now only dawning for the greater part of Christian theologians. I mean this to be taken not as an accusation but as a statement of fact. It could not be otherwise, given the historical development of Christian theology. To pour new wine now into the old wine-skins is reprehensible, but the same did not hold true when they were brand new.

The role of fundamental theology, therefore, is to also work out the intelligibility of theology outside the culture and even the religion where that theology until now grew and prospered. In paradoxical form I would say that if fundamental theology today is to fulfill its role, it cannot be only that of clarifying its own tradition, but it must leave house and kin and wander outside into a *terra incognita,* though a promised land. And here lies the immense difficulty. Fundamental theology is an Exodus theology. But it is not all a question of courage; it is also a query about its feasibility. Is it at all possible to be rooted in an alien or perhaps even non-existent soil? Is it possible to jump, as it were, over one own's shadow?

We should take very seriously the differences among peoples, cultures and religions, for in no other way can the gulf between them be bridged. Today two-thirds of the world's population live in a non-historical dimension; half of mankind does not have the theistic conception of God as the children of Abraham have; one-third of humanity lacks a consciousness of separated individuality. These are some of the many major items of difference that could be named. In a word, the function of fundamental theology consists in providing a theological justification of a theological as well as a religious pluralism.

Metatheology

Fundamental theology becomes rather a kind of *diacritical theology* in the sense that the "diacrisis" was understood in Plato's *Sophist* or "viveka" in Shankara's *Vedanta*. I feel, however, that the simpler term *metatheology* is more apposite, for it seems to suggest a total human attitude transcending, on the one hand, the intellectual elaborations on the message of different religions (theologies) and, on the other, both the "theos" as the subject matter of this attitude and the "logos" as the instrument dealing with it. I am not saying anything against this conception of God or this use of the logos. I am only pleading that God be not taken for granted and the logos divinized. Metatheology could also be described as the human religious endeavor to become aware of, to analyze and or to understand that human primordial relatedness which occurs when dealing with the ultimate problems—an endeavor resulting not out of a particular concept of human nature, but as a fruit of a pluri-theological investigation. I am not assuming that there must be a kind of objectifiable common ground or certain universally formulable common statements. I am only pleading for a really open dialogue—one in which the meeting ground may itself first have to be created—where in the very intermingling of religious currents, ideas and beliefs a more powerful stream of light, service and better understanding will emerge. I only foresee (and in a way prophesy) an earnest religious struggle, an authentic human commerce and intercourse in the deepest level of man, a fruit of love—and not of lust or ambition—pregnant with the good news of a new creature. The Christian surely should not be afraid of being born again, nor for that matter should the adherent of other religions. Nor should any faith shun the genuine search for truth. The confidence in truth is already a fundamental religious category.

The Understanding of the Christian Kerygma

Two important ideas seem to derive from what has been said so far. The first is the need for a radical change in the orientation of fundamental theology itself—in other words, its conversion or *metanoia*. From an internal Christian point of view, I would put it in a manner that is almost the opposite of the usual one (though I should like to add at once that by this divergent formulation I am being most traditional, because tradition has been mostly paradoxical and has actually followed this road on several occasions in the past). I should say, then, that the role of fundamental theology is not that of finding out some extra-theological principles on which its speculation is based, but of showing that the Christian message may become meaningful in any authentic

human attitude and genuine philosophical position, of proving
that the Christian *kerygma* is not in principle tied down to any
particular philosophical system or cultural scheme, or even to
any particular religious tradition. Its role is to explain for instance, not simply that the acceptance of the existence of God is a
necessary prerequisite to understand and accept the Christian
faith, but also that under the hypothesis of there being no God, if
this is existentially given, the Christian proclamation could look
for a justification and a meaning. Metatheology is not just another system of theology, as metaphysics is not simply a more
refined physical science. A theological system may still be theistic. Metatheology does not need to be so, and may be, for instance, at the origin of a non-theistic theological reflection. It
does not encroach upon the different systems or jeopardize the
several theological schools of the most disparate systems and
religions. And yet it belongs to the theological investigation. In
fact, it modifies both the underlying system and the Christian
understanding, though not according to any preconceived pattern,
but as the very result of the metatheological activity itself.

I could clarify this idea from a double perspective. From a
speculative angle I could say that fundamental theology tries to
understand the fundamental theological issue (Christ, for the
Christian faith) in a given philosophical, religious and cultural
situation. From a pastoral and Christian angle, I would add that
it tries to do and say in another context what Christ did and said
in the place and time in which he lived. But this is not possible if
you do not make yourself understood. And again this can only
happen to the extent that you share in the assumptions of the
people with whom and for whom you speak.

The Ecclesial and Dialogical Character

The second idea has already announced itself. It is the com-
munitarian or ecclesial character of this enterprise. It cannot be
the work of Christians alone, or of "religious" people exclusively,
but has to result from the common effort of all those interested
(or "condemned", as Fichte would have put it, though I should

prefer to say "called upon") in performing this major work of dialogue, communication and communion, even in spite of and through the conflicts that may arise.

Here is where theology and religion meet, where life and speculation encounter one another and where the scholar is the wiser the simpler he is as a man. Any one side or party cannot lay out the rules of the game or fix the conditions or the outcome of the experience. Fundamental theology becomes lived religion, mystical faith (because it is previous to or beyond any formulation). It is the religious quest for a ground of understanding, for a common concern, which has to be lived, delimited and verbalized. It is a dialogue which transcends the logos, which begins by being a "dia-logos", a "going through the logos", piercing the logos, as it were, in order to decide which logos we are going to use and if the ground of our search belongs in any way to the logos or to the Spirit.

It is methodologically wrong to start, for instance, by saying that the stumbling block for a Christian-Hindu dialogue is the denial of the personal character of the divine. In the same way, it is equally inaccurate to say at the outset that unless one reaches the level of an all-pervading attributeless Brahman (considered as the highest possible religious awareness) there is no possible encounter of Hinduism with the other world religions.

What I am aiming at is this: to state that the dialogue is not simply a device for the discussion or clarification of different opinions, but that it is in itself a religious category, that it becomes an act of religion, an act of faith (which comes from hearing), a mutual recognition of our human condition, and thus constitutive interrelatedness.

If the aim of fundamental theology is to elaborate the assumptions on which any possible theology is based, it necessarily requires dialogue on equal footing, with the collaboration and the positive contribution of the "others". Only others can help me to find out my presuppositions and the underlying principles of my science. Stated simply, "das Ungedachte", the unthought, can be disclosed only by him who does not "think" like me; he helps me to discover the unthought magma out of which my thinking crystallizes, and I, on my part, can do him the same service.

This procedure throws us all into the arms of one another. The amount of risk and good faith that it requires is patent. It is really a religious act, full of faith, hope and love. But it is also a methodological need. If I have to dig out a foundation on which the other can also stand, I need his help so that he may at least be able to tell me if the ground I find is also a ground for him.

I need his interpretation of myself and of my theology in order to understand myself and my theology; he needs the same from me. Fundamental theology is not an esoteric science or a discipline *ad usum delphinis;* it is the forum of a worldwide *ecclesia,* of all those people for whom the care for the other is as sacred as the preoccupation for their own household. I shall never be able to love my neighbor as myself if I do not know him as my *self*. This sentence obviously applies both ways. The middle ground where we meet is the basis for fundamental theology and also the ground for human encounter.

Heinrich Fries/*Munich, West Germany*

From Apologetics to Fundamental Theology

I

Apologetics comes from the Greek word *apologia,* which originally had the broad meaning of "giving an account of one's own position". In the course of history, however, the theological discipline of apologetics became narrower in scope. It came to regard itself as the justification of one's own position and the rebuttal of another's position. This conception was most clearly evident during the centuries of inter-confessional dispute. Imbedded within a Christian culture and social order, apologetics felt that its task was to vindicate one's own denominational beliefs and to point up the error in the position of other Christian confessions.

The social order of that day was still Christian. Belief in God and Christianity was taken for granted. Against this backdrop, each denomination felt it had to articulate and stress the inter-confessional differences. Only by polemic and debate, presumably, could it preserve and reconfirm the truth of its own faith.

Today, however, neither belief in God nor Christian adherence can be presumed from the start. Both are subject to questioning and radical doubt. If Christian denominations and their theologians were to remain engaged in the narrow confines of polemical debate against each other, then they would be acting very anachronistically, and the understandable reaction of many

57

people would be: "The theological differences in question here belong to a past age. I don't understand them. They don't interest me at all. They're not even serious questions, as far as I am concerned."

By the same token, theologians can no longer treat men's real fundamental questions as they were often treated in the past. They cannot tackle them "apologetically", regarding them as error, apostasy or sinfulness. They cannot devote their efforts to rebutting these questions. If they did, then they would run the risk of rejecting questions whose seriousness and import had not even been appreciated.

Today the main concern is not to rebut error. It is to create a basis for discussion, to open up doors, to listen and ask questions, and to seek answers to these questions.

One of the characteristics of the old-style apologetics was that it regarded the truth it was defending as an unassailable fortress. In the course of vindicating this truth, it proposed to shore up the inner defenses of its home fort. This led to greater conciseness, to be sure, but it also led to greater isolation.

The old-style apologetics sees the opposing side simply as an alien, divisive force that is inimical to one's own position. It does not ask itself whether there might be points of common agreement, nor does it see the possibility that the other side might pose some valid and unanswered questions to one's own position.

By virtue of its approach and methodology, the old-style apologetics is mainly concerned to "objectivize" its own profession of faith and that of the other side. In other words, it seeks to articulate both positions in neat formulas and theses, so that they can be handled more easily. This involves the danger of not giving due consideration to the personal decision involved in the act of faith or to the person of the believer. It also involves the danger that the believer himself is made part of the antagonistic conceptual picture. As a result, there is often a tendency to turn the opposing party into a straw man, so that he can be torn down more easily.

An attack on someone else's position is usually a counterattack. In other words, we let the other person set the theme, and then we simply react to what he has said. Our response is not made from the depths of our own belief or in real dialogue with the other person, but in deliberate opposition to him. Such an approach is ultimately based on an optimistic confidence in the power of proofs and demonstrations, a confidence that is much questioned today. Underlying it is the attitude that only lack of intelligence or deliberate ill will could reject the validity of our demonstration.

This attitude forgets that faith itself would mean nothing if it were simply the result of clear-cut proofs and demonstrations. It is worlds apart from another legitimate function of faith: the possibility of pondering the faith, making it understandable, and working out answers to the question which man himself represents.

II

Today apologetics sees itself as fundamental theology. It regards its course in history as a shift from defending a particular position to laying down a foundation of fundamental principles. It is convinced that only this positive work on fundamentals can provide answers to men's questions. Only within the context of an overall foundation can discussion and debate have a legitimate function.

This foundation is offered because the fundamental principles are no longer presupposed and taken for granted, as they once were; they must be explicitated and developed. It is also offered because today's human beings cannot be approached primarily by challenge and debate. They will open up only if their questions are taken seriously, only if they are shown understanding and invited to dialogue, only if doors are opened to them, only if reality and concrete experience are faced squarely.

The theological discipline of fundamental theology, which deals with the foundations of the faith, must be integrated into this context. Foundations here mean the basic presuppositions which show that faith is possible, that it is a serious question, and that it may provide the answers men are looking for.

When we talk about the foundations of the Christian faith, we can mean two things. I shall consider the first meaning here, focusing on the central issue. Faith only becomes credible when we are clear on the question of Jesus Christ: Who is he, and what are we to make of his claims to be the way, the truth, and the life? We are faced with the Bible's question: "What do you think of the Christ? Whose son is he?" (Mt. 22, 41). Is he just another person? Or is he the one who can say: "I am he" (Jn. 8, 28)?

In earlier times apologists could say that Christ's miracles and the fulfilled prophecies indicated and proved the credibility of the Christian faith, that they clearly showed the divine origin of the revelation happening. Now, in the context of the modern critical outlook, these very proofs have become problematical, and they pose difficulties for the faith. They are not insoluble problems, but their probative value is not what it used to be. This is even more true of other items, such as this statement from Vatican Council I: "The Church herself is a great and constant basis of credibility, and a witness to her divine mission, by virtue of her wondrous diffusion, her conspicuous holiness, her inexhaustible fruitfulness, her catholic unity, and her unassailable perdurance" (DS 3013).

Exploring the foundations of the faith—that is, the conditions which make Christian faith possible—is a task that cannot be put aside, for it involved the why and wherefore of faith in God and Jesus Christ and in the nature and validity of Christ's mission. Although many specific questions are involved here, it should be possible for us to work up a presentation of the overall nature and the specific cast of the Christian faith.

The overall cast of the Christian faith is basically very simple. Therefore, we should be able to say clearly, in a few sentences, what the Christian faith is, and what is the main point and center toward which everything else converges. This can be further differentiated and expanded by more specific questions, to be sure, but it should not become irrelevant or be displaced, even temporarily, by such questions.

We can find such attempts to summarize the Christian profession of faith. In the New Testament, Paul tells the Romans to "confess with thy mouth that Jesus is the Lord, and believe in thy heart that God has raised him from the dead" (Rom. 10, 9). Describing their approach to faith, Paul reminds the Thessalonians "how you turned to God from idols, to serve the living and true God, and to await from heaven Jesus, his Son, whom he raised from the dead, who had delivered us from the wrath to come" (1 Thess. 1, 9-10). In its *Decree on the Missionary Activity of the Church,* Vatican Council II notes that the believer must "realize that, drawn away from sin, he is being introduced into the mystery of the love of God who is calling him to enter into a personal relationship with himself in Christ" (n. 13). Karl Rahner has also attempted to provide a "brief summary" of the Christian faith for the present day.[1]

Such attempts to spell out the foundations of the faith in a theological way are part of fundamental theology.

III

We can also mean something else when we talk about the foundations of the faith, and this second meaning is particularly important and urgent today. It is based on this simple consideration: the object and content of faith (whatever it is to be) and the act of faith itself are possible only if they have a real intrinsic and primeval connection with man and his reality.

In man himself we must find the pre-conditions that make faith a real possibility. The tenets of faith must strike man in such a way that he is real in them and finds himself in an authentic encounter. In this encounter, man should really come to

[1] *Schriften zur Theologie* VIII (Einsiedeln-Zürich-Cologne, 1967), pp. 159ff. G. Friedrich, P. Brunner, K. Lehmann, J. Ratzinger, *Veraltetes Glaubensbekenntnis?* (Regensburg, 1968).

understand himself; he should find his "self" and the answers to his questions. Otherwise, faith is simply ideology.

Examination of the human preconditions for faith is also a topic for fundamental theology, insofar as the latter is concerned with the foundations of the faith. The first item here is to point out that the Christian faith presupposes certain things in man and that the act of faith and its execution fit in with the basic attributes of man. When we say this, we do not mean that faith is a preliminary stage of knowledge or a replacement for it. We mean rather, that faith is one of man's basic possibilities and actions—insofar as it essentially means "I believe in *you*," and not "I believe *that*."

Faith is the way in which I encounter a person and enter into communion with him, the way in which I move out of myself and come to rely on another. It is also the way in which I can come to know another person at his deepest level. I gain this access to another person only insofar as he reveals himself to me. That he can do this is a sign that he is free and capable of communicating himself, and if he does do this, it is an expression of his love.

One person is not at the disposal of another person. Man lives on faith, in this sense, in the sphere of human and personal relations. It is marked by encounter and communion between you and me, and it manifests itself in words, love and trust. Faith, as encounter with another and as commitment to him, is the foundation for faith as belief in a specific content. What is revealed to us in encounter (as insight, orientation, promise) is taken over and accepted in faith.

It is essentially this sort of process that provides access to faith in the religious and Christian sense, for it removes faith from the trammels of a false relationship (e.g., inimical debate) or an erroneous perspective (e.g., faith as a substitute for knowledge). When faith is erroneously construed as a substitute for knowledge, it necessarily becomes more constricted as the scope of our knowledge broadens, it dies slowly from strangulation.

What we said of human faith is also true of faith in God and

Christian faith. It is not primarily a belief in theses or specific tenets; it is belief in a person, a "thou". It opens us up to a reality which is of critical importance to our existence, but which could not have been glimpsed or penetrated in any other way. It is not a superfluous addendum to our life, but something which touches our very core and gives meaning to our existence.

We move from interpersonal faith to faith in God as we come to see how much God is part of the picture for man. As Rudolf Bultmann has put it: "To speak of man is to speak of God." [2] God belongs somewhere in the definition of man; thus if a person disavows God he ultimately misconstrues man (Herbert Braun).

Today, of course, talking about God is not something that comes easily or that can be taken for granted. We cannot presuppose God at the start of our reflections, as if no one would question that presupposition.[3] Moreover, we cannot presume at the outset that we can move from the temporal world to the eternal God, as the classic proofs for God's existence assumed. Today the world seems to be more the work of man than the work of some creator whose trademark it bears.

Now this does not mean that contemporary man has no access to the reality we call God. But today man finds this access to God in himself and in self-reflection. Man experiences unconditioned responsibility, absolute dictates of conscience, radical self-surrender and love. He encounters the consolation of trust, the call to reconciliation and the obligation of universal brotherhood. He comes to realize that he is at the disposal of another, that he is indebted to another for many gifts, that he is the recipient more than the author of many things. In suffering, tragedy and death he experiences his limitations and his passivity.

All these experiences point man to a beyond outside himself. It is not a geographical "beyond" out there, but a beyond that is "present in the very midst of human life" (Dietrich Bonhoeffer). It approaches us unconditionally (Paul Tillich), and we meet it

[2] R. Bultmann, *Welchen Sinn hat es von Gott zu reden?* (Tübingen, 1933), pp. 26-37.

[3] Cf. H. Schultz (ed.), *Wer ist das eigentlich, Gott?* (Munich, 1969).

as soon as we are courageous enough to stop running away from ourselves.

Thus interpersonal human faith does not and cannot provide us with an absolute, unconditional belief in another, even though it points us in that direction. This absolute claim upon man, which represents the very core of man himself, cannot be subsumed under the attributes of the human person as such. It cannot be ranged alongside human autonomy, freedom, love, self-communication and self-revelation.

IV

The reality of God is suggested to man in the phenomena mentioned above. But they exhaust neither God's capabilities nor the reality of man. We cannot say that it is not possible for man to experience further encounters or communications from God. Why? Because man is an open-ended being with no sharply defined limits. The unlimited nature of his questioning process indicates this. Behind his questions there always lies something further toward which they are pointed.

Now, this means that the religions of the world, as expressions of man's orientations toward God, are markedly ambivalent, ambiguous and vague—not to mention the fact that they can be abuses of religion. Conscience, too, as summons and response (G. Ebeling), is ever open to a more concrete articulation and a more decisive word; this is especially true because man often "holds back" (Rom. 1, 18) and falsifies the truth which conscience provides. Finally, we must note the mute dumbness which man faces in the most decisive questions of his existence. All these experiences transform man into a listener, open to yet another word from himself or someone else and waiting expectantly for it.

If there is to be some divine self-disclosure for man, it can only come in the realm of history, for history is the realm of the other, the new, the unexpected, the free action. Moreover, this new "divine revelation" can only come through words. It is through words that reality is pointed out. It is through words that communication is made possible, that encounter and community are created, that the person is summoned. And only a person can transmit such a revelation.

To be sure, we are not saying that such a new revelation in history is thereby proven or made inevitable. Its content and its carrying out are not to be presumed or anticipated. But we are saying that man does have access to this reality we call God, and to some new self-disclosure from God, in history, through words.

Man, of his very nature, has access to the basic teaching of the Christian faith: that this new revelation found its ultimate expression in the concrete history of Jesus of Nazareth. Man has access to this teaching because history is always a concrete slice of history, because man is always pointed toward a concrete here and now in which he must make decisions and live out his life. He must opt for a person, for an action, for a duty, for a way of life.

Man lives in history, caught between the tension of past and future, tradition and uncertainty. His own inner capabilities will not provide him with the answer to the deepest questions confronting him. He must resolve these questions *a posteriori,* by confronting history and what it has to tell him. Taking cognizance of this predicament, man finds himself confronted with the Jesus-happening in history. He is summoned to respond to the challenge laid down by Jesus; he must make a decision.

We are often advised not to commit ourselves to anything or anyone, to remain aloof and avoid making a decision. But we may and must opt for one specific person or one particular event in history, if this one particular person or event gives us a view of the whole, if from this one we can grasp everything and attain full freedom.[4] But that is precisely what the Christian profession

[4] Cf. B. Welte, *Heilsverständnis* (Freiburg-Basel-Vienna, 1966), esp. pp. 216-26.

is: that the exclusive claim embodied in Jesus is of universal dimensions, that it embraces the whole.

V

Christianity tells us to opt for Jesus in the welter of temporal and human history, to choose him out of all the religions available. This option could never be made simply by an analysis of the available possibilities. No complex of reasons or motives can eliminate the necessity for faith. But when we do opt for Jesus, we need not shun the justification for this choice. For in his person and deeds, Jesus is far different from the prophets and founders of other religions. The distinctive nature of the Christian message is based on the distinctive nature of Christ, and we can describe this distinctiveness.

By the same token, however, we find in Jesus the unique embodiment and fulfillment of characteristics that radically typify man—i.e., his grounding in God, the summons to give himself to God and the world, and acceptance of the world. Pilate's words "Behold the man" (Jn. 19, 5) apply to Jesus as they apply to no other human being. The truth of this statement is brought home fully when man allows himself to be plunged into the reality that Jesus represents, when he commits himself to the imitation of Christ.

Earlier we noted Bultmann's phrase: "To speak of man means to speak of God." If we turn this phrase around, we shall complete the picture: To speak of God is to speak of man as he really is. The God of Christian belief is the God who is radically associated with man, the God who provides the definitive answer on the nature of man and the purpose of his existence.[5] This does not mean that God is nothing more than an aspect or function of man's self-questioning; if he were, he would not be God at all. It means that only God and his Word can tell us who this

[5] Cf. H. Bouillard, *Logik des Glaubens* (Freiburg-Basel-Vienna, 1966).

open-ended, questioning being (man) is. And the God in question is specifically the God of Abraham, Isaac and Jacob, the Father of Jesus Christ, the God who approaches man as a brother in Jesus Christ.

Everything that God does in salvation history has a relationship to man. Through it, man is to come to know who he is and to turn the world into a human reality. The content of the Christian faith is meant to tell us who man is and what his existence means. As St. Paul puts it: "Making known the truth, we commend ourselves to every man's conscience" (2 Cor. 4, 2).

What is the difference between the believer and the unbeliever? It is not that the former accepts things uncritically while the latter does not; it is simply that the former does not reject the Christian faith out of hand, but allows it to encounter him as the decisive reality and summons. It is not that the believer has blind faith while the unbeliever opts for intellectual honesty; it is that the unbeliever chooses [6] to remain skeptical, to avoid opting for anyone or anything, while the believer makes a responsible option for faith and tries to make it a real part of his life.

These brief reflections have not covered the whole field. To be complete, we would have to say that man, of himself, also has access to something called the Church, where this faith is transmitted and communicated. Why? Because man is also pointed toward transmitted tradition, community and interrelationship.

VI

In closing, we should note that the questions confronted here are of the utmost ecumenical relevance. They relate to faith in God and the overall Christian message, rather than to issues that divide Christians. They are questions of radical importance today, and the answers must be worked out jointly by all Chris-

[6] Cf. K. Rahner, *Intellektuelle Redlichkeit und christlicher Glaube* (*Schriften zur Theologie* VII) (1966), pp. 54-76.

tians. We must seek the truth together, and theologians can and must contribute the insights of their own particular denomination. It is a first-class ecumenical opportunity.[7]

More is to be gained here by working on a common task toward a common goal than by focusing on our denominational differences in an ecumenical spirit. This is not to say that the latter task has become superfluous. It simply means that it has taken on broader dimensions.

This concentrated ecumenical effort in fundamental theology would involve a real competition with the pluralistic answers provided by philosophy and other religions to man's most fundamental questions. It is a competition we should not fear or shun. The true test is: Which set of answers convincingly engages the full dimensions of man and his world? This is the test that will separate faith from ideology.

[7] Cf. H. Fries, *Die Herausforderung des Glaubens durch die säkularisierte Welt* (Munich, 1968), pp. 181-202.

Juan Segundo, S.J./*Montevideo, Uruguay*

Fundamental Theology and Dialogue

I f fundamental theology means, in general, the study of the possible conditions under which God can have spoken to men and men have recognized, listened to and accepted his Word, then, paradoxically, one can say both that this problem has come to dominate the whole of theology, and that fundamental theology is in the process of disappearing.

Fundamental theology, leaving aside its epistemological definition—that is its proper aim, limits and methods—plays an important part in the training of a priest, occupying no less than a year of his studies. And it is highly significant that this year is often presented to the future priest as that of "Church and world problems".

In effect, compared with the *dogmatic* subjects of later years, fundamental theology, just because it is *fundamental*, seems like a sort of border zone in which it is possible to dialogue with non-believers on a plane of equality, using similar instruments of logic and language. Once the portals of dogmatic theology are reached and fundamental theology is left behind, on the other hand, the lines are cut and we enter the territory of language comprehensible only to the initiated, arguments that cannot be resolved by common sense—a world, in fact, not shared with the rest of men.

Whatever the best solution to this problem, it seems to me to pose a basic question: What are the frontiers on which the Church debates with the world, with what *epoché*—that is, without which elements of theology? More particularly, is the theology we call fundamental capable of serving the dialogue with non-believers?

I

SOCIO-THEOLOGICAL OBSERVATIONS

If one is willing to excuse the pomposity of this heading, I think such observations can bring a useful approach to the problem. I should like to try and reconstruct the atmosphere of that year devoted almost entirely to the task that may conveniently be summed up in the title of one of the main treatises in fundamental theology: the examination of "true religion". One must logically think that a whole year devoted to the examination of such a subject would suppose the recognition of proving the possibility of such a thing beyond all reasonable doubt. It would hardly be possible for such a lengthy study—and one called "fundamental" at that—to lead to the forming of a mere opinion, with as much chance of being right as any other. One therefore had to assume that intelligences, in other ways often superior to those of our teachers, were obfuscated by continual distractions or overtenacious prejudices.

I particularly recall—the case has a demonstrative value—the proposition put forward one day by one of my fellow students: "Would it not be possible to arrange for all heads of government to meet at the U.N. and spend a few days discussing the questions that we have been studying? Then, if there's anything in all this, they would all be bound to agree and so leave the religious question settled once and for all."

I remember that the idea seemed mad enough at the time, half paranoic even, simply because the general atmosphere had left me very skeptical about the "efficacious" demonstrative value of such arguments. But I did not then recognize the *theological* implications of the idea and how wide of the mark they were. What it in fact implied was the "human" possibility of declaring Christianity to be true before knowing what it said—and this while recognizing the fact that great thinkers, apparently sincere, held that what it said was damaging to humanity.

One did not need to be a great theologian even then to know that the "excellence of the doctrine put forward" had to occupy the first place in the dialogue that brought a man to the faith. Nevertheless, through some strange requirement of logic, one had to start by establishing, with copious and often unclear historical arguments, the veracity of the gospels, the divinity of Christ, his intention to found a Church, and that definitely the Roman Church, the power given to the said Roman Church to interpret his Word correctly, and so on and so forth. From then on the "Word" defined authoritatively by the Roman Church, whatever it might say, logically had to be held to be true.

This experience, which was no more than a continuation of that undergone by our elders, produced the following "theoretical" pastoral schema: there are two main functions: (1) to inform the faithful, in more or less summary form, about dogmatic and moral theology, on the basis of the word of an authority already accepted in faith, and, later, to furnish educated Catholics with an apologetic arsenal useless to them but invaluable for facing up to the infidel; (2) the function of "evangelizing"— i.e., presenting the historical message of Jesus to non-believers.

Now, it was evident in practice that this division of labors— into dogma for believers so that they could be saved, and into fundamental theology for unbelievers so that they would be evangelized—could never exist except as theory. Anyone with a smattering of culture who had the choice between listening to fundamental theology or going away chose the latter. Even when, through the efforts of Labertonnière, Blondel and others, a more "immanent" way of putting it across was found, it was still not possible to avoid speaking of Christianity "in bulk", and with the risk that each and every expression used to allude to it was already tainted by a stale theology vaguely spread about and just as vaguely understood.

Thus evangelization became a "theoretical" task for the Church, an occupation for Christian philosophers or some charismatic preacher or retreat-giver. In practice, the Church as *sent* to non-believers lacked a pastoral training in preparation for faith. There was one decisive point in the schema: how to get *authority* accepted? Before that point was reached, no one really knew what to talk about. Once it had been passed, it didn't really matter very much what one talked about, because by then one believed everything *en bloc*.

Another, more recent example was provided by a seminarian in a catechetical course who commented that he had attended a "brilliant" series of lectures on the central dogmatic themes— the Trinity, grace, redemption—and added, "It's not the sort of thing one can talk about, of course—but brilliant." The scheme of things again: fundamental theology must be communicable to non-believers (because they do not accept authority); dogmatic theology does not have to be communicable to non-believers because it is directed at believers (who accept it on authority).

I should like to draw the attention of non Latin American readers to the real significance of this pastoral schema. I believe it exists in Europe, but there it is overlaid by the context of a Church rich in different functions, and particularly in lay people who think about their faith in relation to their worldly commitments. But in a poor Church, swept under by demands for a "popular religion", the pastoral fact of a generic acceptance of "what the Church teaches"—that is, of the authority of the Church—becomes crucial.[1] Once this point is reached, the pas-

[1] On this aspect of the Latin American situation, I should like to refer the reader to my contribution to the joint work: B. Catão, J. Comblin, S. Croatto, G. Gutiérrez and J. Segundo, *Salvación y construcción del mundo* (Santiago/Barcelona, 1968). This article will shortly appear in English in *From Society to Theology. A Latin American Essay.*

toral counseling of the faithful can stop; until it is reached, there seems to be no way of approaching the concept of faith.

II
DIALOGUE AND DOGMATIC THEOLOGY

As I see it, Vatican Council II clarified an essential point which completely destroys the foregoing schema: dialogue with non-believers is realized with what properly constitutes dogmatic theology.

Briefly, one can say that any statement belonging to revelation is as much a statement about God as about human history (*Constitution on the Church in the Modern World*, n. 22). The God we know is the God of love, and we only know him as actually loving in history, as intervening—that is, in a history whose origin, end and law is love (*ibid.*, nn. 38 and 22).

We also know that the love that proceeds from God was given to all men (*ibid.*, n. 24) and is at work in the whole history of mankind (*ibid.*, n. 22). In a more or less instinctive or immediate fashion, man has always been capable of loving, of giving himself, of participating in the paschal mystery of Christ, from the beginning. But as hominization proceeded, the problems occasioned by love became detached from their instinctive immediacy and were situated on the level of a deeper and more mediate reflection (*ibid.*, n. 23). This was the historical moment God chose to bring his revelation to a head and hand it over to his Church. Those who receive this message about the very history of humanity in faith (*ibid.*, n. 15) see in it a solution to the human problems brought about by good will—that is, by love (*ibid.*, n. 11). Furthermore, faith is only given as a means of finding these solutions, not as a magic formula for finding one's own salvation through formulating it in an orthodox manner before God.

This is where the paradox comes in: while it is true that faith is an *absolute*, in the history of mankind it is subordinated to another *superior* truth, one which is practical and builds up humanity, one which has to be found in a dialogue to which all men bring their experiences, their questions and their answers (*ibid.*, n. 16).

From this it follows that because Christian truth is not absolute, it can be possessed fully or adequately even while it does not become part of the human solutions required by history, as a realistic control of our true orthodoxy (*ibid.*, n. 19). In other words, revealed truth is not a capital deposit that can produce interest completely on its own, but a message destined to form part of, and be possessed in, a dialogue (*ibid.*, n. 11). It does not give the Christian ready-made solutions, nor does the possession of a truth that comes from God absolve him from the responsibility of seeking the further truth that ends in man and in his history (*ibid.*, n. 16).

The dialogue that justifies the very fact of revelation will thus take place between non-believers and believers on the basis of those human problems that arise from the building-up of history (*ibid.*, n. 3). If it is successful, this will be because the absolute truth that came from God will have passed, through the believer, in the form of a creative element in the formation of absolute perspectives on a more profound, more universal, richer, more viable and future-orientated view than if this element had been missing.

And this is precisely what we mean by the *Good News*—a persistent, tenacious, ever-new piece of Good News related, in each problem, to every vicissitude of history (*Constitution on the Church,* n. 35). In a way, to use a political simile, Vatican Council II replaced the "once and for all evangelization of the individual" by the "permanent evangelization of mankind", in much the same way as Trotsky opposed the doctrine of the "permanent revolution" to Stalin's doctrine of finishing the "revolution in one country" before passing on to the next.

In reality, this permanent evangelization should not be confused with individual conversions to Christianity. Nevertheless, the latter will, to the extent determined by God, be the consequence of the former, *and not the other way around,* because each solution found by love constitutes a "preparation for the Gospel" (*ibid.,* n. 16). It is, in fact, of prime importance for God's plan for the whole of human history that the progress of love should not be held back for lack of that element of response which he confided to his Church.[2]

This is the leavening function of the Church which, according to Vatican Council II, is the whole reason for her existence (*Constitution on the Church in the Modern World,* n. 40). It obviously consists not in converting the whole mass of dough into leaven, but in changing the texture of the whole mass, through a "hidden" number of men who place revelation at the service of human problems and their solution, and so come to know and to hold revelation always anew, guided by the Spirit. Let us not fear to say that the Church has no other mission (*ibid.,* n 42). If she had, the fact that she was founded after a million years of mankind's hard, uncertain, stumbling progress would be the greatest nonsense of all.[3]

In this scheme of things, which we might call *permanent evangelization,* dialogue is not carried on up to the portals of dogma, but from the very center of dogma itself. It is therefore not fundamental theology that is charged with establishing this dialogue which is the focus of the mission of the Church *sent* to the world, but *dogmatic* theology.

III
A STEP BACKWARD

This is why I cannot help considering the theological basis of a certain document (which is otherwise welcome and encouraging) a step backward. I refer to the document produced by the Roman Secretariat for Dialogue with Non-Believers. This doc-

[2] Cf. my *Teología abierta para el laico adulto:* Vol. I, *Esa Comunidad llamada Iglesia* (Buenos Aires, 1968), Ch. III.
[3] *Ibid.,* second general note to Ch. IV.

ument sets up a supposed divergence between Paul VI's *Ecclesiam Suam* and the *Constitution on the Church in the Modern World:* "In the encyclical *Ecclesiam Suam,* Paul VI deals at length with dialogue from the *apostolic* point of view: it is through dialogue understood in this way that the Church carries out her *main task,* which is the *announcement of the Gospel* to all men so as to offer them, with respect and love, *the gift of the truth* and grace of which Christ has made her the custodian. In the Pastoral Constitution on the Church in the Modern World, *the emphasis is rather on the dialogue between the Church and the world: this dialogue is not directly aimed at the announcement of the Gospel.* This is precisely the dialogue which Christians try to establish with men who are not of the same faith, either to seek the truth together in various fields, or to collaborate in solving the great problems of mankind today. It is to dialogue understood in this way that the following remarks apply. . . ." (italics mine) [4]

Here the definition of each of these two types of dialogue follows from the supposed distinction drawn between them: in the first, truth is found ready-made in the Christian who passes it on to anyone willing to listen to it, and this is the main task of the Church; in the second, truth is not possessed by one side or the other as they are, because the subject is composed of various problems that belong to the world, and in seeking a common solution to these problems rather than the truth, Christians are not exercising an apostolic function, let alone carrying out the prime evangelizing function of the Church.[5]

[4] This is the document signed by Cardinal König as president and Vincenzo Miano as Secretary, *Il Regno. Docum. Catt.* (Oct. 15, 1968). As for the interpretation it makes of the concept of dialogue in the *Constitution on the Church in the Modern World,* let us admit not the ambiguity of the texts, but the fact that texts produced by differing concepts are set side by side. On the principles of interpretation to be applied in such cases, cf. my *op. cit.* Vol. II: *Dimensiones de la existencia cristiana,* general note to Ch. III.

[5] This is not a reason to fear, as has been noted, without giving equal consideration to its theological basis, denying the opportuneness and need for, and even the legitimacy of dialogue when, as happens in the majority of cases, it has been "instrumentalized" in the intention of the person taking part. This would not apply in the case of evangelizing apostolic dialogue.

For me this is a pre-conciliar theology and to the scheme of fundamental theology I discussed at the beginning of this article. It is characteristic that in neither of the two types of dialogue mentioned in the document is there any mention of dogmatic theology. It does not come into the first, because this is a matter of bringing the Gospel to non-believers, nor into the second, because this is a discussion of various problems arising from the state of the world today. Dogmatic theology remains a realm *ad intra* not concerned in dialogue. It is the truth we possess whose portals man approaches through the arguments that are supposed to make it credible.[6] Thus fundamental theology, reduced like this to a process of "apostolic" proselytism, languishes, and evangelization becomes more and more detached from a secular world.

IV
THE CONCILIAR SCHEMA

Now, if we replace this schema by what seems to be that of Vatican Council II, dogmatic theology should take on the task of conducting the dialogue essential to the Church's mission in the world, guided by clearly defined conditions that speak to that *epoché* or reduction referred to earlier. The reader will think of the problem of language here, but I consider the problem of a common language to be a secondary one that largely disappears in the wider context of another, more specifically theological task.

The example I gave earlier—namely, of the "brilliant" treatise on the Trinity or grace that was not something one could talk

[6] I have already shown why I see this problem as essential for pastoral approaches in Latin America. But it is hard for the pastoral theology of this continent to make its voice heard. When a high dignitary of the Secretariat put forward this schema at a meeting of theologians in Santiago, Chile (presided over by the secretary of CELAM, Msgr. McGrath y Pironio), practically all those present declared themselves opposed to the theology underlying the document. Nevertheless, Fr. Miano told *Inf. Cath. Int.* (Oct. 15, 1968): "No objection has been made, either at the doctrinal level, or at any other."

about—revealed a theological difficulty rather than a linguistic one; it was a difficulty in understanding the revealed message. Faced with political problems, for example, the extent to which personal creativity should be given rein will either be a subject for dialogue or not, where Christians are concerned, depending on whether or not they have received and understood the revelation of the Trinity and grace. If a study of the latter does not seem like Good News to those who are trying to build a more creative society, then theology will have been badly understood and we will be—even though we formulate it traditionally —faced with a "heterodoxy" such as Vatican Council II mentions in the particular case of our image of God (*ibid.*, 19).

This is not the place to discuss the dogmatic methodology that should allow the kernel of the message to enter into dialogue with non-believers in building up history. This is clearly a huge task. People talk of *demythologization* as a legitimate exercise in *suspicion*. One can in fact suspect that a theology which does not "evangelize" through the problems of history has let itself be caught up in heterogeneous and extraneous elements. I would consider this task, carried out unilaterally and accentuated by secularization—or, rather, impelled by a secularization containing many elements that lead to impoverishment of social life, particularly in a capitalist society— to be one particularly suited to wealthy societies and one that should not be widespread without qualifications.

On a continent like Latin America, theology still has time to carry out the dual function it will require for dialogue. This is to combine *demythologization* as an exercise in *suspicion* with *remythologization* as an exercise in *restoration* of the meaning of the message.[7]

---

[7] P. Ricouer, "L'unité profonde de la démystification et de la rémythisation du discours ne peut apparaître qu'au terme d'une ascèse de la réflexion, au course de laquelle le débat qui dramatise le champ hermeneutique sera devenu une discipline de penser," in *De l'interpretation. Essai sur Freud* (Paris, 1965), p. 61. The whole of Vol. I of this work contains valid theological insights throughout. For its underlying aim, let this quotation suffice: "Ce qui est implicite à cette attente, c'est une confiance dans le langage; c'est la croyance que le langage qui porte les

The problem of making the authority of the Church acceptable *en bloc*—and, by the same token, the problem of fundamental theology—thus becomes either an anthropological pro-
pedeutic, or a complementary and continual investigation of
dogmatic theology itself. This must occupy the central place in
dialogue with the non-believer.

---

symboles est moins parlé par les hommes que parlé aux hommes, que les
hommes sont nés au sein du langage, au milieu de la lumière du *logos* qui
éclaire tout homme venant au monde. C'est cette attente . . . qui anime
toute ma recherche" (p. 38).

Jan Walgave, O.P./*Louvain, Belgium*

The Essence of Modern Fundamental Theology

I t is impossible to speak intelligibly about the purpose and method of a modern fundamental theology without first explaining what this expression "fundamental theology" means. We understand by this the attempt of Christian thought to justify the acceptance of the faith. But this "justification of the faith" can mean two different things: it may mean that I try to form my own judgment for my own conscience, and this I can do without referring to any controversies; or I may concentrate on the objections made by others, in which case there may be no connection with my own personal faith.

These two approaches to apologetics are clearly distinct. But, though distinct, they cannot be completely separated. Since my life is necessarily a life with others in a common world, my thought can hardly disentangle itself from every dialogue or discussion. The mentality which produces the problems of our age penetrates every one of us and, if ignored, can have serious repercussions on our own life of faith.

Therefore, fundamental theology has a double task. It must gather and coordinate all that contributes to make the Christian

81

message acceptable to man, and it must erase the objections which make the message look unacceptable.

The Function of Fundamental Theology

The new mentality of today and a new look at the theological past have brought the Christian world to accept fairly generally that it is in no sense the function of fundamental theology to "prove" the truth of the Christian message. All that is expected of it is that it should deal with the reasons which can justify the acceptance of the faith as a moral option for a serious conscience.

The Nature of the Arguments

This view leads to a radical change in our thought about the nature of the arguments which are relevant to the kind of demonstration that fundamental theology should provide. The old apologetic rationalism only accepted arguments that were based on undeniable facts and as such could be shown to be objective: miracles, fulfillment of prophecies, etc. The so-called "internal arguments", based on the aspirations of the human soul, were considered purely subjective and as such either rejected or tolerated as incidental considerations.

Today the situation is rather the reverse. The historically-based "demonstration" is today often relegated to some intellectual limbo or allowed to appear on the fringe of the "real" demonstration, as incidental matter. The reason for this change lies mainly in the renewed theology of faith. Even more than was the case with the Fathers of the Church, it is now stressed that as an existential event the faith contains all it needs for its certainty. But this event takes place nevertheless in the context of an existence which already understands itself in some way and can analyze this understanding by reflecting upon it. This self-understanding cannot by itself create the faith in us, but we can nevertheless establish a certain agreement between the two.

M. Blondel, who was the first to uphold the value of such a method based on immanence, subjected the extrinsic approach of the old apologetics to devastating criticism. To believe, according to Blondel, is a personal act, and in order to justify this act of mine I am presented with historical theses and arguments which can only be judged by scholars and which unbelieving scholars contradict with impressive counterarguments. In this controversial situation I can only choose blindly: "They pretend to base the religion which is said to be the only way to salvation on a knowledge which only few enjoy; they make the faith depend on proofs which I have no means of checking myself." [1]

In 1929 and 1930 *Nouvelle Revue Théologique* published three articles which showed that, according to the experiences of people involved in the apostolate, it is not learned arguments but the Christian phenomenon itself which creates in man that disposition which normally precedes belief and accompanies it.[2] Following up H. Bremond's study of Newman's psychology of faith, Blondel had already suggested that even the protagonists of extrinsic apologetics "based their arguments in reality, though unwittingly, on better reasons which influenced them vaguely, although they could not recognize them or make explicit use of them." [3] It became therefore a matter of analyzing the reasons which are already operative in the spontaneous conscious life of man before he begins to reflect upon them. The attempts made in this direction show, as is to be expected, a fair amount of convergence and divergence. But the general idea had already been felicitously expressed by Cardinal Dechamps: "There are only two facts to verify, one inside you and one outside you. They both tend to unite, and of both, you yourself are the witness." [4]

In the past much emphasis was placed on the objective, extrinsic facts: the Church, with her sanctity, her unity, her catholicity,

[1] M. Blondel (writing under the pseudonym of François), "Raisons de ne pas croire," in *Oeuvres de Laberthonnière. Critique du laïcisme* (Paris, 1948), p. 296.

[2] The authors of these articles were E. Przywara, P. Charles and H. de Lubac.

[3] See Blondel, *op. cit.,* p. 296.

[4] V. A. Dechamps, *Opera Omnia* I, pp. 16 and 428.

her loyalty to the apostolic past, and her beneficent influence on society and in every sphere of life, or Christian doctrine, with its beauty and cohesion, its moral nobility, its historical continuity, and its influence on thought, art and literature.

Today many of these arguments no longer impress modern man. He is rather inclined to admit that the Church, though holy in Christ for the believer, nevertheless shows herself only too sinful in her representatives and members. The herosim of love, which, through Christ, inspired so many saints, remains impressive. But there are also noble and heroic souls outside the faith. Is Gandhi not just as impressive a figure of saintly love and selflessness as many of the great Christians venerated in the Church? Moreover, the moral controversies of today have convinced many Christians that an atheist can be just as good and generous as a believer.

This leaves us, then, to confront the Christian message with the deepened self-understanding of man and the philosophy which analyzes the motives that live in that self-understanding. I wish to emphasize once again that this confrontation, which is to be analyzed by fundamental theology, is something existential, pre-reflective, and therefore already in being before reflection is applied. Within this framework reflection thus has only a clarifying, analyzing function. The function of fundamental theology is therefore to stimulate awareness, and its method is evidently Socratic. The theologian must himself participate fully in the experience which he describes and analyzes.

Sin and Redemption

This theme is as old as Christianity itself. Moreover, awareness of the existential paradox into which sin has landed us is so deep and so universal that in all religions of the world it makes man look for some way of redemption. There are different views about the nature, the cause and the solution of this unfortunate situation, but the awareness that this radical experience of unhappiness is somehow linked up with self-seeking is wholly universal. According to Buddhism, self-seeking can only be overcome by excluding the self. According to Christianity it is overcome by a conversion which creates in us the possibility of selfless love once again. This requires God's forgiveness, and that forgiveness is given to us through Christ who, in his incarnation and death on the cross, revealed to us the depth of God's love. In this way he also presented us with the radical demand that we should be a "person-for-others".

Here I want to add three observations:

1. The encounter between the confused conscience and the message of salvation can only be authentically translated into life by an alert conscience. Therefore, if fundamental theology wants to be relevant, it must also find the way toward this awakening of man's conscience so that its voice can be heard in man's purified self-understanding.

2. However, man's pride resists this. He prefers to deceive himself and to see in sin merely an imperfection which self-training can overcome both in the individual and in society. Hence the Christian Socrates or "physician of the soul" must develop the art of dialogue which he can only acquire through a long and honest interrogation of his own heart.

3. Within the perspective of secular thought, God gave man an historic mission to fulfill which is ultimately ethical and which relies exclusively on man's freedom and ability. He must therefore undertake this mission without counting on God. He can also solve his ethical problems without special help from God. By paving the way to a better world in a responsible manner, ethical disorder will also disappear in the end. It is true that man has been entrusted with a noble historical task which he can only achieve himself in positive cooperation with God. But this idea does not logically imply that the will, which must execute this task, can find in itself the inviolate moral power required for it. It lies in man's power to achieve whatever he can do on the basis of science and technique, and thus by a positive intervention. However, there is no technique which can produce a deepening of

man's good will, and this has been and still is evident to all who
have reached genuine maturity and a true self-understanding.

The Transitory Condition and Salvation

This theme, too, is as old as conscious life itself. Many of the
oldest religions (Egyptian) were already based on the experience
that man's transitory condition robs his conscious existence of all
meaning. The hope of a fulfillment which snatches us from the
grip of this transitoriness is, consciously or unconsciously, one of
the existential conditions that make man's life possible.

Modern man wants to assert unconditionally the value of his
task within this world, a task directed toward the achievement of
a more perfect humanization in our relations with each other.
Our culture tends toward a salvation which must be brought
about by man himself within this world. This salvation is a community where all forms of alienation that divide us are abolished
and where our mastery of nature is put at the service of an unsel-
fish commitment of all to all. Therefore, the question is whether
our hopeful idea of being on the way toward a salvation in this
world does not turn into its dialectic opposite if our culture as a
whole is destined to perish in this transitoriness and is therefore
ultimately meaningless. The question here is not so much my
own disappearance as the meaning of the whole undertaking in
which I wish to cooperate unselfishly. "By the nature of this
undertaking there is total incompatibility between a total death,
which would hurt and ultimately abolish our consciousness on
the one hand, and conscious activity on the other, since it would
break the spring of this activity." [5] S. Toulmin and S. Ogden [6]
have pointed out that although technological and scientific activity and moral activity each have their own non-religious norm, a
communal undertaking nevertheless presupposes a total confidence in an ultimate and lasting meaningfulness. To man, threat-

[5] Teilhard de Chardin, *Le phénomène humain* (Paris, 1955), pp.
255-57.
[6] S. Toulmin, *An Examination of the Place of Reason in Ethics* (Cam-
bridge, 1950); Schubert Ogden, *The Reality of God* (London, [4]1967).

ened by despair, neither science nor morality can, of their own, offer a basis for this confidence. It is the function of religion and theology to interpret the basis of this confidence, which makes life possible and which lies at the source of life, before there is any reflection on it. Religion therefore presents itself to the whole of man's cultural undertaking as the answer to its inherent eschatological question.

Which religious answer to the question of man's existence is the most satisfying and the most acceptable? Christianity is a message that speaks of the approaching "kingdom of God" and an invitation to extend that kingdom, inaugurated by Christ, here on this earth. This kingdom of God is a living community in which God makes himself God for us and in which we live our humanity in him by being human for each other. Thus, in its striving toward an earthly incarnation, the aim of the kingdom of God is partially identical with the object of that hope which animates our culture. The "penultimate character" (Bonhoeffer) of salvation within this world is based on the "ultimate character" of communion in love with God, and this wrests salvation in this world from the threat of transitoriness. Is it not possible that the escape from the tyranny of the self through communion with one's fellow man is ultimately based on communion with the source of love which gave rise to the universe and the whole cultural movement? Must a consistent humanistic "secularity" not exclude "secularism" because the "saeculum" (transitory time) becomes ultimately meaningless in "secularism"?

Christian Philosophy

Today attempts are being made to work out more objectively what it is that confirms the credibility of what lies within this confrontation of man and revelation. Christian thought has here a double task: on the one hand, it must methodically clarify the inner cohesion of revealed truth (theology), and, on the other, it must explain the experience of man's existence in the light of this truth (Christian philosophy). In brief, all thinking is by nature

directed toward the provision of the most acceptable and satisfying cohesive view of the data of experience so that we can orien-
tate our conscious life accordingly. Every science proceeds with
data of experience and "thinking models" or "hypotheses" which
serve to organize these data into such a synthesis that their cohesion and meaning become clear (intelligibility) without leaving
any significant fact unexplained (comprehensiveness). Now, revelation offers a coherent whole of ideas which claim to provide a
satisfactory answer to the ultimate and most characteristic questions of man's existence. Would the "Abrahamic presupposition"
(Hodges) then not be the one to enable us to gather the experience of existence together in an intelligible pattern in the most
acceptable and comprehensive manner? [7]

M. Blondel's "catholic philosophy" clearly links up with this
Christian philosophy, which the Anglican Church in particular
has developed so well. If, says Blondel, philosophy is radically
true to its function and method, it is bound to discover that it
cannot find the answer to its own ultimate problem in itself.
From the vantage point of his own problems, the philosopher can
nevertheless see and judge that the "mysteries" of the Christian
revelation, though they cannot be proved in themselves philo-
sophically, do in fact provide the true and satisfactory solution
for the "riddles" in which all thinking about the basic issue of
philosophy necessarily results.

Conscience and Church

Newman's argument about conscience starts from the existence of providence. Within this perspective he asks what the conditions are under which the human conscience, which constitutes
man's existence and therefore already precedes any reflection as
the root of all thinking, can express itself purely in its own right
in our reflective existence and develop itself there honestly.

[7] This Christian philosophy, already initiated by F. Schlegel and L.
Bautain, is very popular today in England. It is linked with such names
as W. Temple, J. V. Langmead Casserley, H. A. Hodges, E. Lewis, L.
Hodgson and others.

Man's conscience is dialectically confronted with the sinful world which tries to stifle the voice of conscience by the impersonal and social statements that this world takes for granted. Should we then not expect God's providence to come to the assistance of the conscience by calling into being a power of a social nature which dares to tackle the world on its own ground and overcome it? This social power is then, according to him, the visible Church founded on Christ and God's Word. Normally, thought can only respond to the conscience when the God-obscuring power of the world of sin is constantly neutralized by the illuminating power of a visible world of grace.

Newman knew just as well as Kierkegaard that the Church's divine light can be temporarily obscured in the visible institution of the Church. Her members and leaders still belong to the "world of sin", and her pollution constantly threatens to lead to a worldly compromise or a "conventional Christendom" which is rooted neither in the conscience nor in the Gospel. That is why the Church constitutes an enduring concern for Christians. She loses her persuasive power to the extent to which she is absorbed by the world of sin.

The Emphasis on Practice

This brings us to a last motive. Whether the Church is credible or incredible for modern man depends, first of all, on her living appearance here and now. It is simply not good enough to point to her beneficent influence in bygone days or to prove theoretically that the salvation which she preaches can embrace and promote earthly salvation in principle. The Church must prove herself in the situation in which we live today. God's Word is creative. Therefore the word of the Church among us will only appear divine if it changes the world creatively. "Whether the Word succeeds in reality in what it claims theologically must be judged by its power with regard to the temporal world, in the sense of a creative fullness of power over time. . . . The Word has this fullness of power when it is spoken to the present world—i.e., when it really introduces man into the present situation by illuminating and changing it." [8]

Difficulties and Objections

It also pertains to fundamental theology to tackle contemporary difficulties and objections on their own ground. In this regard I would like to formulate a few principles:

1. Every theoretical interpretation, even in the exact sciences, frequently has to face very serious difficulties. No scientist sees there a reason to throw his conviction overboard. For instance, upholders of the theory of evolution are not shocked in their "faith" by the fact that there are biological and anthropological difficulties for which they have no answer. Thus there is, from the purely human point of view, no reason to reject the Christian interpretation of the world because there are difficulties which we cannot solve satisfactorily. This principle of apologetics is strongly brought out particularly in English thought.[9]

2. The Christian need not let himself be treated as an inferior creature who has no point of view of his own and must always obey the latest fashion in matters of science or philosophy. One does not have to be a great historian to know that the very development of a science solves all kinds of difficulties within this science. Newman has analyzed this attitude of peaceful autonomy in the faith with outstanding wisdom in the last chapter of his *Apologia*.

3. The deadly sin of a modern thinking man is apparently one-sidedness or bias. Scientific facts, interpreted in a special way, are used by biased scientists to project a vision of the world which is in fact based on unconscious philosophical principles, and so we are given not a scientific theory, but a philosophical interpretation. Here fundamental theology must sort out what is

[8] G. Ebeling, "Zeit und Wort," in *Das Zeitproblem im 20 Jahrhundert* (Bern, 1964), p. 357. The same idea also occurs in H. Cox, Ian T. Ramsey and E. Schillebeeckx.

[9] This is typically English and goes back to Bishop Butler's *Analogy of Religion* (1736).

scientific fact and what is philosophical prejudice in such statements. This is the best way of clearing many so-called scientific difficulties out of the way. This method was successfully worked out by the Dutch philosopher H. Dooyeweerd and his followers and applied to concrete cases.

Joseph Cahill, S.J./*Notre Dame, Indiana*

A Fundamental Theology
of Our Time

An investigation of some thirty-two Fundamental Theology textbooks has made it clear to me that there really was no general consensus as to the nature and properties of a theology that was called fundamental or basic. Some authors describe the subject as if it were purely a philosophical approach to establish and justify the nature of Christianity as a revealed religion. Other writers thought that fundamental theology was a properly theological endeavor because it employed the light of faith, even though in a negative way. The results of these theoretical ambiguities manifest themselves in the restructuring of many seminary curricula available to the author. There is a current tendency to eliminate fundamental theology and to substitute in its stead courses in Scripture or other courses of seemingly more modern relevance and appeal. In view of this very concrete reaction which will undoubtedly affect the theology of the future, I should like to discuss first of all the failure of fundamental theology, to describe some characterisitics of a modern fundamental theology, and finally to propose a definition of fundamental theology—one large enough to encompass both present and future needs.

The Failure of Fundamental Theology

The initial failure of our present fundamental theology (its structure and contents go back to John Perrone's works pub-

93

lished from 1835 to 1842) sprang from the fact that the discipline attempted to do too much; it extended itself beyond its com-
petence. Witness, for example, the naive and uncritical treatment
of Scripture in the fundamental theology textbooks. Even apart
from the overly polemic tone and intent of traditional fundamental theology, there was the further weakness of parochialism. By
and large the subject confined itself to an already believing community. Ecumenism, a pluralistic world and the crisis of faith
today have made that parochial approach unsuited and uncon-
genial to the modern mentality. Finally, the growth of sciences
such as history, archaeology, psychology, biology, psychiatry,
sociology and philosophy, as recognized universes of discourse
which say something about who and what man is, even in his
relation to the transcendent, has made traditional fundamental
theology obsolescent. For in recent years fundamental theology,
which basically dealt with religious meaning, has been subject to
competitors in the cosmos of religious meaning. The scope of traditional fundamental theology was to assert that God had
revealed, confirmed his revelation by prodigies, and founded a
Church. Man, consequently, was to accept the fact of revelation
and its ecclesiastical custodian if he wished to live under the
canopy of religious meaning. The highly developed sciences of
today, especially the social sciences, are in many instances inimical if not hostile to a revelation coming from outside of man.
Even the neutral sciences, however, do propose respectable alternatives to the options proclaimed in fundamental theology.

Universality and Immanence of Revelation

This brief critique brings us perhaps to an adequate beginning
point for a description of a more pertinent fundamental theology.
Fundamental theology today must be the opposite of a concept
of God speaking to man totally from the outside and completely
in the past. Revelation (if we must keep this concept) and salvation should be construed as processes that occur via the grace of
God, but as much from within man and the social community as
from outside of man. This statement will find its foundation and

theological justification in a theory of the presence of Christ in the world today. If present, he is therefore operative, whether one chooses to describe this activity in terms of Christ or his Spirit. Such a theology, of course, has not by any means been elaborated. But if the theory is correct, then we must admit that Christ (or the Spirit) is operating in the world today. Fundamental theology will escape its narrow parochial confines if it seeks to enucleate when and where and how and with what necessity God is operative within the human community today. Criteria of discernment are neither easily nor mechanically available. Fundamental theology will, moreover, have to base itself on the large and sound theological principle that God wills all men to be saved. And if this is the case, then the fundamental theologian cannot simply speak of a past and exclusive revelatory event but one that can and is taking place here and now.

To go further, fundamental theology must take up the question of precisely how God operates in the world and how he is active within men. It is fully possible, given the universal salvific will of God, that he operates in society by what we might call the social conscience of the merging community. And it is equally possible that he is present in the gradual refinement of the individual conscience. If so, then the fundamental theologian has a sound basis for at least attempting to describe an immanent revelation and salvation. Moreover, it is very likely that God can operate effectively outside of what we would call organizational Churches or ecclesial communities. The discernment of these possibilities and the analysis of man as capable of receiving God's revelation and salvation in the above manners is a primary task of fundamental theology today. Admittedly this leaves, if not the fundamental theologian, then certainly the ecclesiologist with the delicate task of explaining the relation of the Church to salvation and to the world.

To return for a moment to the question of the immanence of revelation, we must say that the fundamental theologian must outline some metaphysics of belief where revelation occurs and is accepted by man and the social community because man is a spiritual being and as such is open to the activity of the spiritual being that we call God. In a world which today asks the question "Is there a God?" the fundamental theologian must have some coherent explanation of the existence of this God through his operation in man and in his world. It is at this point that fundamental theology will take up the question of the coherence of God's current activity with the events described in Sacred Scripture.

The complexity of the above operations indicate that the fundamental theologian can no longer operate in a vacuum. Somehow or other he must be in dialogue with psychology and psychiatry and the social sciences. He must be in a position to learn from the practitioners of these sciences whether or not there is a verifiable religious *a priori* in man. If there is such a thing as divine activity, then one might suppose that traces of the divine would be found in man and in his history. But the limitations of time, talent and training demand that the fundamental theologian work in concert with other disciplines. The task will not be easy because it demands reorganization not only of the theological enterprise but also of many of our institutions. The most evident place in which this intellectual investigation may take place is the community of interpretation that is supposed to be found in the university. A further presupposition of this procedure is the existence of dialogue in the sense given to it by Josiah Royce. The dialogue would be a mutual discussion in which something brand new, something totally unforeseen emerges. In this sense there is no substitute for the dialogue which is both the cause and the condition of new learning.

The Central and the Peripheral

It has been pointed out by several writers on our subject that fundamental theology cannot afford to bother itself exclusively with historical questions of a recondite but irrelevant nature. For fundamental theology is essentially an historical discipline which, to be effective, must operate in what might be called the history of the present moment. As an historical discipline the historicity of fundamental theology is determined by the awareness, the choices, the decisions of the theologian as he is historically determined. On the second level, fundamental theology is historical in that it develops in a concrete culture and ethos which are not the same at every period of world history or in every country even of the same historical period. Thus the fundamental theologian must become an interpreter—an interpreter of himself, of his culture, of his contemporaries, and of God's self-communication. Put another way, the fundamental theologian must ask the question, "What is currently urgent, given the culture and world in which I operate? What deserves priority?" At all periods of the Judaeo-Christian civilization the central element has been that God somehow or other communicates himself. It is the contemporary self-communication of God with which the fundamental theologian should be concerned.

More concretely, it may be noted that the pressing point in 1969 is not the intellectual integrity or the highly structured organism of the Church. It is safe to say that Americans today look to the Church to find goodness. Hence the fundamental theologian may well serve as the critic of the Churches which do not manifest the goodness and love of God. Intellectual arguments about the papacy or the magisterium or the Church will be as effective as the goodness, righteousness, mercy and kindness that men can see in the Church and ecclesial communities. In this light it might be said that the fundamental theologian, insofar as possible, will exercise a role parallel to that of the prophets in the Hebrew Scriptures.

A Modest Discipline

Fundamental theology will be a modest discipline—modest in the sense that no one theologian or generation of theologians will ever be able to remove or diminish the ultimate mystery of the transcendent God. The overly rationalistic character of traditional fundamental theology almost made faith the inevitable result of a syllogism and thus denigrated the mystery of God as well as the quality of faith as a free gift. But more than this, fundamental theology will be modest in its realization that today no one world view has a monopoly on truth. And thus fundamental theology will be much more open to the wisdoms of this world which do, as a matter of fact, seek to give some meaning and intelligibility to man's existence on earth.

The Bible

If we spoke above about fundamental theology distinguishing the central from the peripheral and being at the same time a modest discipline, then we must also say that fundamental theology will be much more biblical in the future. For if we hold that all revelation is contained in the Bible and in its interpretation, then the fundamental theologian must speak with an awareness that the Bible is relevant to the concerns and cares and status of modern man. Concern for the poor and the needy, concern for social justice, love of neighbor, sacrifice—all of these are issues as modern today as at the time the books of the Bible were composed. A return to the Bible should likewise make certain that the theologian does not set up human laws or demands as divine and thus substitute idols for the transcendent God. Nonetheless the fundamental theologian must be cautioned that not everything in the Bible is relevant to all periods. Consequently, once again the fundamental theologian must appear in his role as interpreter—interpreter of the texts which have peculiar meaning and relevance for the age, the culture, the country, the world in which he finds himself.

Toward a Definition

Thus far we have indicated some of the tasks and qualities of fundamental theology. These characteristics might assume a more concrete dimension if we made some attempt to describe the nature of the theological discipline.

Fundamental theology has always had an apologetic intent—i.e., it has always sought to make the Word of God intelligible and acceptable. In the Hebrew Scriptures the Israelites are always seeking to interpret the promises of Yahweh and to make these promises comprehensible in the light of each generation's peculiar historical problems. The Deuteronomist, for example, begins with a direct theological reflection on the covenant. From the abstract theological reflection the author proceeds to persuade his contemporaries to obey the covenant. Even in exile he affirms that Yahweh is just, and on this premise he seeks to base the hope of the people. At times his efforts seem unconvincing. But his work is in the broad area of religious persuasion. He attempts to relate the promises and demands of the covenant to individuals in a concrete historical moment. He has the enormous task of reconciling the destruction of the temple and the exile itself with the promises of the covenant relationship. But let it be noted here that this attempted reconciliation presumes a certain prior theological reflection and comprehension.

The New Testament likewise is an apologetic book, one that seeks to make the demand for faith both intelligible and acceptable. Each of the books bears the stamp of the author's interests as well as the audiences' concerns. There is no doubt that each of the contributors to the New Testament is a theologian, and it is from their theological reflection that their apologetic or persuasive concern emanates. The reaction of each writer in the New Testament is a diverse reaction to one and the same saving event; therefore, it is true to affirm that the books of the New Testament are hermeneutical books, works of interpretation characterized by the theology of the authors, determined by the needs of specific historical audiences and shaped by the intention of the writers to exercise religious persuasion.

Now, while we might show the same interests and concerns among the Fathers and early writers of the Church as well as during the period of the Reformation, it is enough to note attributes common to all who have engaged in the apologetic function of fundamental theology.

First of all, fundamental theology is a necessary by-product of a more general theological understanding. Hence if we say that theology is a habit and one possesses the habit when he can rather easily formulate his own questions, answers and terms, then it would seem that fundamental theology is a particular use of the more general habit of theology. This particular use of the habit of theology has the very definite goal of giving a relevant explanation of the demand for faith (and, one might even add today, the demand for hope). The effort of fundamental theology is in the direction of religious persuasion. The object of the persuasive effort is what we have called the demand for faith, which is concretely the demand for faith and belief in the person of Christ. This Christian demand for faith specifies a personal dimension, a relation of one personal being to another personal being. It is not the theologian or the Church but God himself who makes the Christian demand for faith. The objective dimension and pole is God himself and his chosen means of self-communication. This objective pole is primarily the term of speculative theology. The subjective dimension and pole is the intelligent, willing, historical man subject to God's self-communication. Fundamental theology is determined by this contextual bi-polarity. In order for persuasion to be effective, it is supposed that the fundamental theologian will have an adequate grasp of both poles.

Some Distinctions

Here it may be worthwhile to draw some distinctions between speculative theology and that use of the habit which we have termed fundamental theology.

The habit of speculative theology exists in the speculative intellect; it is a good of the intellect. The use of the habit exists primarily in the practical intellect and is directed toward the good of the will. Speculative theology seeks intelligibility. It exists in the objective, theoretical order where man inevitably asks what is the thing in itself. The use of the habit seeks credibility in the more subjective, practical, historical order where man asks what is the thing in relation to himself. Speculative theology is an ascending movement to system, theory, notions, the abstract and the transcendent. The use of the habit is a descending movement to the singular, the real, the concrete, the temporal individual. Thus the use of the habit exists in the world of intersubjectivity. Speculative theology seeks a notional assent in the speculative order and is religious by context. The use of the habit seeks a real assent in the world of decision and is religious in itself. Speculative theology ascends through all the data of positive theology to that which is prior in itself. The descending movement of fundamental theology is to the contemporary situation in all its contingency and complexity. For this reason it is highly doubtful that there will ever be a permanent and definitive form of fundamental theology.

This use of the habit of theology is directed to the existential man in the historical now. Since the demand for faith is directed to all men of all historical periods, fundamental theology seeks to relate the demand to the here-and-now, concrete, individual man with all the growth and development of past history, in his present human situation, in his own cultural climate, ethos and orientation. The existential man is the individual in all his singularity, limitations, gifts, desires and weaknesses—man as much created by the civilization in which he lives as by his own personal activities. The historical now in which fundamental theology must operate is the character and climate of the time in which the existential man lives and which must inevitably modify not only the individual and the social community but also the fundamental theologian. Thus fundamental theology might be described as a continual dialogue conditioned by the theologian, the man and community to whom he is speaking, and the history in which they all find themselves.

Karl Rahner, S.J./*Münster, West Germany*

Pluralism in Theology and the Oneness of the Church's Profession of Faith

The theme of this article is a very topical one today. The pluralism of theology is making itself felt in the concrete life of the Church, particularly when this theology is not viewed in narrow Scholastic terms. Church authorities and the faithful are confronted with urgent questions: How can any genuine oneness of credal profession be maintained in the face of this pluralism? What does such oneness involve? How can it be distinguished from pluralistic interpretations and be preserved along with a legitimate pluralism in theology?

The problem is a new one. It is a real *quaestio disputata*. As yet we have not seen the problem clearly enough to work out a clear answer to it, or even to provide an answer that would be generally acceptable and that would resolve the practical difficulties it poses to Church life.

No one would expect me to cover all the aspects of the problem in this article. I myself realize that I am caught in the middle of it, and that I have not resolved it to my own satisfaction. My outlook is still a fragmentary one, and my approaches to an answer are still very much open to question. Upon closer inspection, they may even turn out to be erroneous.

However, one of the consequences of our pluralistic theological situation is that a man cannot go off into a corner and quietly let a fully rounded answer take shape in his mind. He must have the courage to think out loud, in public, before he can offer a simple and clear answer. This may explain why my thoughts are presented here in a more personal tone than they ordinarily would be in a learned article.

I

A New Situation

First of all, and most importantly, we must realize that present theological pluralism presents *a real problem,* and that it is *a new problem.* Both these facts are often overlooked or bypassed by professional theologians themselves. Why? Because the professional theologian knows that there have always been different schools of theological thought in history, that theologians have not always shared the same opinions on a given issue, and that the Church has fostered theological diversity by defending controversial theses against charges of heresy or heterodoxy.

Knowing these things, a theologian might well be inclined to see nothing new in the theological pluralism of today. He might feel that such pluralism has always been around, that the Church and her magisterium long ago worked out sound guidelines and procedures to handle this situation, and that she has been able to foster theological diversity while preserving the oneness of her credal profession.

But here appearances are deceiving. The quantitative increase in theological pluralism over the centuries has produced, as it were, a qualitative mutation. The present pluralism is quite different from the old pluralism. If one does not recognize and admit this fact, he cannot appreciate the real problem facing us today. He will fail to see the new difficulty which the Church has in preserving the oneness of her credal profession.

The Old Pluralism

What was the general situation in olden days? There were schools of theological thought and different tendencies, of course. To some extent, however, they were divided along geographical lines and separated by a cultural no-man's land (e.g., the Eastern and Western Church Fathers). To some extent, the differences and variations among them were not taken into conscious account. When these differences were noted and challenged head-on, the opposing views usually confronted each other as black and white within an overall context of shared presuppositions, concepts and focal questions. Even if later historians might dispute the extent of this shared framework, the differences were not adverted to by the schools that engaged in these debates.

In the old days, a person could operate on the assumption that he knew the position of the other side. He understood the other's position and he could explain why he did not accept it. When agreement could not be reached within this context of real (or presumed) mutual understanding, people shrugged their shoulders and accepted this simply as a fact. If any explanation was offered for the failure to reach an agreement, it alluded to the difficulty of the material in question or (usually) to the stupidity of other theologians and the malevolence of the heretic.

In any case, people operated on one of two convictions. Either they knew what their theological opponent was saying and understood him, or else they didn't even know that there was a theological opposition around. Either they shared the same terminology, philosophical presuppositions, speech world and outlook on life, or else they did not advert to whatever differences were present.

The New Pluralism

Today the situation is radically different. Many factors have contributed to this qualitative change, and they cannot all be analyzed closely here. The historical material, on which the theological disciplines must work, has become so enormous that the individual theologian cannot master it all, and the theologian himself now realizes this. Moreover, the methodology of the various disciplines has become so complicated that no individual theologian can handle them all. The theologian must use philosophy in his work, but philosophy itself has become so pluralistic that no single theologian has *the* philosophy. He must work with some specific philosophy, however eclectic it may be.

Unlike former days, philosophy is no longer the one market place where theology picks up relevant information about man from his whole cultural life and from other scholarly disciplines. The modern disciplines of scholarship (the natural sciences, the social sciences and the history of ideas) have emancipated themselves, rightly or wrongly, from philosophy. The theologian should maintain direct contact with all these disciplines. This is almost impossible to do in practice, unless one chooses to believe that what he does not know about them is theologically irrelevant.

Any Catholic theology today finds itself in a completely new dialogical relationship with other Christian theologies of an exegetical, historical and systematic nature. It is no longer a simple yes or no relationship, because the theological lines of division now cut across denominational lines. The resultant theological pluralism cannot be overcome by teamwork either, no matter how necessary it may be and how intensively it may be organized. No team can embrace all the theologians in the world.

The cognitive process in theology and other liberal arts, moreover, differs from that in technology and the natural sciences. In the latter disciplines, conclusions and findings can be taken over and adopted as ready-made. In the former disciplines, by contrast, the personal cognitive process itself is a pre-condition for the proper understanding and appreciation of the conclusions reached. That is another reason why teamwork cannot resolve the problem of theological pluralism.

Today not even the basic outlines of every possible theology can be retained in the mind of the individual theologian. This, too, is a new situation, and the theologian is well aware of it. Knowing that he cannot know everything around, his personal theology seems fragile and open to question.

The new theological pluralism described here does not involve a confrontation between clearly contradictory theologies. If such were the case, the principle of contradiction could be invoked to show that a thing cannot be true and not true at the same time. When a person can regard two positions as clearly contradictory alternatives, he is in a position to make some basic option with regard to them. The contradictory nature of the alternatives allows him to surmount the pluralism he sees.

The pluralism we face today, however, does not provide us with a set of clearly contradictory alternatives. Theologians cannot find some higher ground, outside both alternatives but common to both, from which they may pass judgment on both. Nor do they possess a common framework of mutual understanding, within which they might start a debate over specific theses. Nor is it possible for theologians on either side to tell each other exactly where their basic frameworks of understanding differ. All they know is that there are differences, because they feel a trace of strangeness in their encounter. The other party seems to move from a different starting point or to introduce different material; his presuppositions seem strange to me, or less important than my own. The dialogue breaks off in mid-air, because it cannot go any further.

The Theologian's Existential Problem

To make clear what I have been talking about, let me take a more personal tack. Here I speak from experience. An older theologian, born and bred in the old Scholastic tradition which reigned pretty much up to Vatican Council II, finds it difficult to understand what I have been describing. How have we older theologians gone about our business?

Well, if we were not the sharpest people in the world or were overly impressed with the absolutes of Scholastic theology, we found the assertions of other theologies to be alien or somewhat strange. We rejected them as false or, at best, unimportant. Without really sensing the objective and existential weight of an opposing position, we found enough reasons and distinctions to "deal with" these opposing positions. The whole problematic involved in our reaction was never consciously adverted to.

If we were smarter and more wide awake, we took a different tack. We revised our basic presuppositions, we broadened the horizons of our understanding, we expanded our terminology, we introduced nuances into our viewpoint and perspective, we learned how to think in terms of modern exegesis and modern philosophies, and we calmly and openly revaluated the changing history of dogma and theology (without losing our sense of continuity). In this way we managed to assimilate much of the seemingly strange data that came to us from other theologies (non-Catholic theologies in particular) and the context of modern existential thought. We made this data a real aspect of our own theology.

Now this latter approach is certainly legitimate. It bears some fruit, and it should not be given up. But today, I feel, we have come to see the limits of such a procedure. Alien ideas are close to us, and we can see them as such. Yet we cannot relate them to our own system, or legitimately reject them as being false or one-sided. Today we often find it impossible to adopt a clear-cut stance toward someone else's basic theological position, especially (but not only!) when he belongs to another Christian denomination.

When one of these alien theologies explicitly and directly rejects some obligatory teaching of the Church's magisterium, then we have a relatively easy time of it. We can, at the very least, pronounce a definite no against his rejection. But then the gnawing questions begin: Did our opponent really understand the magisterial teaching he was opposing, or was he merely rejecting a false interpretation of it? Have we orthodox theologians understood and explicitated the magisterial teaching in such a clear-cut way that we can expect our opponent to have understood us and to accept our viewpoint?

But this particular case is not the real crux of our present dilemma in dealing with alien ideas. We are encountering basic positions, held by alien theologians, which do not spring from a shared horizon of fundamental understanding and which do not directly contradict our own theology. The disparity is not clear-cut, so that we cannot tackle it directly. In such cases we cannot adopt a clear yes or no toward the other side.

Examples

Who among us can say for sure whether the basic conception of Barth's doctrine of justification is Catholic or not? If someone feels that he can, I would like to shake his hand. But where do we go, if we cannot even do that?

Who can say for sure that the ultimate root positions of Rudolf Bultmann are really un-Catholic? Who can say that the ultimate conclusions to be drawn from the postulates of the Bultmann school actually undercut his real intention and are unacceptable to Catholics, whether the Bultmann school realizes it or not? What do we do if we are not in a position to form some clear and responsible stance toward the other positions which confront us?

We run away from the real problem when we say that we should leave the matter alone, when we feel we have done enough by calmly reflecting on our own Christian faith and presenting our theological views to others. We must remember that there are other theologies around which claim to reflect the same profession of faith. It would be simple enough, of course, if we could have our profession of faith without worrying about the disparate theologies. But faith and the theological explication of it cannot be neatly divided off from one another. Therefore, how do we find out what the other person's profession is when we cannot understand his theology or come to terms with it?

Here is a second example. We are all aware of the debate

going on between the Roman and Dutch theologians over the
doctrine of the Eucharist and the explanation of transubstantiation. I for one could not say that the Roman theologians are
less intelligent or less expert than their Dutch counterparts. But I
cannot help feeling that the Roman theologians, with all the
good will in the world, simply cannot follow through on the philosophical presuppositions and the existential ontology that lie
behind a serious doctrine of transignification. The dialogue,
therefore, cannot be fruitful.

Now such an understanding is theoretically possible, of
course. And if we did reach it, we would have to check to see
whether such an interpretation would hold up dogmatically. But
what are we to do if these presuppositions are not present on the
Roman side, or if they are present but not clearly articulated on
the Dutch side? Such a situation is entirely possible, and it is no
reflection on the intelligence of either side or on their desire to
reach mutual understanding. (Look how long it took for the
insights of post-Descartesian philosophy to filter into the
Church's philosophy!) And what are we to do until mutual
understanding of each other's presuppositions and eucharistic
doctrine becomes truly feasible?

Now, one cannot explain the problem away by saying: "Well,
if we establish that these two positions are incommensurable, at
least for the time being, then we have introduced a third position
here. This third position understands both sides and, in making a
judgment on their incompatibility, has created a bridge over
them." The holder of this third position, you see, feels (perhaps
correctly) that he has understood both sides and overcome the
disparity between them. But he must ask himself whether in
other cases he himself is faced with the same inability to follow
through on the other side's position. After all, the two parties in
our present case are convinced that they have really understood
each other's position and have checked it out objectively.

Here is a third and final example. What happens today when a
professional theologian meets an educated Catholic intellectual

who has not been shaped by Scholastic theology but who is interested in theological questions? The theologian often finds that he is faced with an entirely different complex of theological viewpoints, involving fundamental structures and perspectives that are quite different from the ones he is used to.

When the layman begins to speak out of his framework, he will often say things that strike us as outright heresies. We see astonishing *lacunae* in his framework, shortcomings we feel should not be there, and a stress on realities and values that seem secondary to us. The whole framework of his theology has a different cast than the one we would expect to find in any good intellectual Catholic. For we expect that the cast of his theology, shaped by his early catechism training and later religious instruction, will mirror our own theology to a large extent.

That is not the case. Here, too, we confront an alien theology, and we soon realize that we have neither the time nor the ability to reconcile his theology with our own. His alien theology is influenced, even more than ours, by personal experiences in life, by psychological factors, and by his intellectual and social milieu. These conditioning elements are quite different in the life of the professional theologian, and the resultant theological differences are not going to be resolved with a little dialogue or instruction.

This means we must ask ourselves some hard questions when we confront alien theologies. Does the cast of our theology display the same contingent elements that we found in the theology of the Catholic intellectual? Does it contain gaps and loopholes and one-sided emphases that others find shocking? Are we unaware of them because we spend too much time talking to ourselves with a common terminology and within a common horizon of understanding?

When we have honestly faced up to the reality and complexity of the new pluralistic situation, we can try to figure out how to deal with it. This is our crucial question, and the answer will not come easily. The proposal made here will certainly not satisfy all the theoretical and practical problems involved. It is presented, with many personal reservations, in the hope that it may lead to a revision of our thinking.

The Burning Quest for Knowledge

The first thing we must realize is that the present pluralism in theology is not simply a static condition that must be taken for granted. It is a fact that cannot be erased casually; rather, we must do everything we can to overcome it. We must engage in dialogue with every school and line of theological thought. We must critically reexamine our own outlook, broaden our horizons of understanding, and learn as much as we can from others.

The present state of theological pluralism signifies that man's burning quest for knowledge has come into its own. The individual Christian and the theologian want to know more, and the Church's theological awareness has suddenly come of age. Knowing this, the theologian should realize that he cannot simply accept or try to erase the present pluralism in theology. He should realize that it is part of the reality of the human condition, of man's historical and provisional nature. It cannot be overcome once for all time. It is something to be conquered anew every day.

A New Situation for the Magisterium

The second thing we must realize is that the continuing pluralism in theology places the Church's magisterium in a new situation. This certainly does not mean that the Church no longer has the right, through her *sensus fidei* and her magisterium, to draw new and clear-cut boundary lines. Nor does it mean that she cannot, in certain circumstances, reject the teaching of a theologian as heretical or intolerable in the Church. (On what grounds and in what manner she will do this remains to be discussed.) Nor does it mean that the magisterium no longer has the function of declaring something anathema under certain circumstances.

Theological pluralism does not permit us to tolerate anything and everything. Credal profession and theology have a mutual relationship to each other, and they cannot be neatly distinguished from each other in concrete cases; but the oneness of the Church's profession, which makes her what she is, must be maintained in this complex interrelationship. We may gain some psychological, historical or sociological insight into the reasons why someone arrived at a clearly heterodox position, but this does not mean that such a position can be held legitimately in the Church. In rejecting a heterodox position, the Church does not rule out a person's good faith or his chances for salvation; nor does it mean that these heterodox views cannot contribute in a positive way to the further development of the Church's understanding of the faith.

Granting all that, we must still say that the way in which the Church exercises this right and this duty will have to take on a wholly new cast in the light of the new pluralism. This is the real question we are dealing with here. If the Church does take conscious note of the new pluralism, and if she realizes that it cannot be overcome in an instant, how can she reshape her way of preserving the oneness of her profession? It is a new question because the pluralism itself is new and has a bearing on the way in which the Church and her magisterium will preserve the oneness of profession. My comments provide only a fragmentary approach to the answer.

III
THE GRAMMAR OF CHURCH PRONOUNCEMENTS

We cannot tackle the problem of theological pluralism adequately if we do not realize that there is a definite grammar and vocabulary involved in the magisterial formulas which express the Church's profession of faith. This grammar need not have been the one it is. It is not dictated by the doctrine itself; it is influenced by historical, psychological and sociological factors.

Because it involves a deliberate determination and formulation, it deserves our respect. But this respect is not to be equated with our assent in faith to the binding doctrine itself.

The role of grammar and vocabulary in the formulas of the magisterium has not been given much consideration as yet, although we find vague allusions to it here and there. This is not surprising, because in earlier days both sides shared the same speech world or did not advert to the gradual changes taking place in it. As a result, the opposing doctrines were formulated with the same words.

Today, however, we need only reflect on some of the older terms to see that a definite grammar and vocabulary is involved in the dogmatic formulations, and that it need not have been the one it was. Consider the use of "person" and "nature" in christology and the doctrine of the Trinity, and such terms as "original sin" and "transubstantiation". This terminology is not dictated by the doctrine itself. Indeed it becomes a real problem when changes take place in the secular speech world, within which this terminology was used and understood, and when the Church cannot control the linguistic history and development of these concepts.

In the light of this changing linguistic situation, we cannot conceive and practice the oneness of credal profession, the pluralism of theology, and the interrelationship of these two factors as they were conceived and practiced in the past. We cannot operate on the assumption that authentic fundamental statements of *both theology* and credal profession can *only* be found within this grammar and vocabulary. Nor can we any longer assume that the "explanations" of these magisterial concepts, which are necessary and have always been provided, are purely secondary and supplementary commentaries on the real authentic theological statements. These theological commentaries, which were once regarded as secondary comments on the authentic theological corpus of magisterial concepts and theses, can have an entirely different role of importance in today's theologies. They can even form part of the real substantive corpus of theological doctrine.

Let me repeat this in another way. In former days, the statements of the Church's magisterium were the truly important theses of theology. This need not be the case for theology in the future. Indeed, it cannot be the case if theology is to perform its proper task. The grammar and vocabulary of magisterial pronouncements hold primarily for the Church's credal profession; they do not hold, in the same pristine and obligatory way, for theologies as such. To be sure, the theologies have a continuing relationship to the doctrine of the magisterium, and hence to the grammar and vocabulary employed by the magisterium. But today we must realize more clearly than before that it is the grammar of the Church's credal profession more so than the grammar of theology.

In former days, people realized that this grammar had a history that pointed back toward the past, and that it came into being at some point in this history. Today we must also take cognizance of the fact that this grammar also has a history that points toward the future—at least insofar as theology is concerned. (Attempts to present such theological concepts and their grammar as irreplaceable in the future—such as we seem to find in *Humani generis* and *Mysterium fidei*—are neither proper nor convincing.)

Even if some such procedure were proper where our credal

profession was concerned (and we shall come back to this), it does not hold true for theology and theologians. It is the fundamental right of theology as such to express the substance of its teachings, insofar as they are primarily theological, in terms that are different from the formulations of the Church's magisterium. This, of course, does not mean that theology can pass over these official formulations and their grammar in complete silence, or that it is not bound to the real obligatory teaching contained in these formulations.

For example, an updated theology of the Trinity might well explicitate and elucidate the obligatory elements of the Church's teaching without having "three persons" and "one nature" as the central elements. The doctrine of original sin could be expressed in an orthodox and acceptable way, without ever using the term "original *sin*". It could do justice to the teachings of Trent, and it need not obscure the real content of this doctrine any more than the classical formula does. The latter, after all, fails to bring out the purely analogous relationship between personal and inherited habitual sin.

To sum up: there is an element of grammatical influence in the pronouncements of the magisterium, and we now realize this. It shows us clearly that theological pluralism is both possible and justifiable, and that theology can move even further away from the formulations of the magisterium.

IV
CREDAL ONENESS AND THE MAGISTERIUM

Our problem is thus brought into even clearer and sharper focus. How can we ensure the oneness of our credal profession amid this plurality of theological expression?

Greater Trust in Theology and Theologians

Our general predicament is this. On the one hand, our credal profession must be formulated in some specific theological language; even the formulations of the magisterium use theology, a specific theology, to some extent. On the other hand, the commensurability of various theologies—i.e., their convergence toward a unified credal profession—cannot be verified by the individual.

In the light of this situation, and keeping in mind the reservations stipulated above, we would have to say that the Church and her magisterium must give much more room to the individual theologies. She must give them the responsibility of making sure that they remain in accord with the Church's credal profession, and that their interpretations preserve the profession rather than destroy it.

It is clear that the Church's magisterium, too, is faced with the consequences flowing from a pluralistic theological situation. On the one hand, the magisterium may be guided by representatives of a specific theology. On the other hand, it may accord equal weight to the views of widely differing theologies; in this case, the insurmountable pluralistic situation in the Church will be mirrored in the magisterium itself. In either case, the Church must give much more responsibility to the theologies themselves than she has in the past. These theologies must see to it that they preserve our common credal profession.

As we pointed out earlier, it is quite possible that in certain cases the Church's magisterium may have to say that the formulations of a specific theology are incompatible with her profession of faith. But we certainly cannot set down *a priori* norms that would tell us automatically when a theology is using its new-found responsibility correctly and when the magisterium has to step in to challenge heterodoxy.

Even in the latter case, we can assume that it often will involve a matter of grammar and vocabulary rather than a matter of doctrine itself. The magisterium will be defining limits on an epistemological and sociological plane, even though its pronouncement may take the form of a declaration on doctrine itself. In other words, the magisterium will really be saying this: "You cannot talk like this in the Church without endangering your own faith or the faith of others and doing injustice to the doctrine involved." After admonishing the theology in question to respect the grammatical boundaries laid down, the Church will again leave it up to the theology to interpret our credal profession.

Criticism and Pastoral Inspiration instead of Dogmatic Formulations

In the new situation we face, the old credal formulations and magisterial pronouncements may well have a different degree of importance and significance. They were, after all, fashioned in the language of a specific theology, even in the New Testament itself. (Even there, of course, a certain amount of theological pluralism is evident, but it was a pluralism that was not consciously adverted to by those involved.) Yet they do represent a perduring and obligatory starting point and norm (norma *normata*) for later pluralistic theologies, because they were the unique expression of the Church's common profession and helped to preserve the continuity of the Church's *sensus fidei*.

Today the magisterium must still use some theology to express its profession of faith. But now there may be a greater or lesser degree of difference between its credal profession and the theology used to express it, and this difference may be insurmountable. Therefore, we may well have to assume that in the future the magisterium will not be able to formulate new emphatic doctrinal pronouncements. Why? Because the unity of theology, which is a presupposition for such pronouncements, is no longer present. In the future we may expect the magisterium to set limits from time to time, to protect and encourage the various theologies that are trying to give contemporary expression to our credal profession, to view with favor the pluralistic theological situation, and to expand its traditional function by providing occasional pastoral directives that will guide the Church, in a prophetic and evangelical way, through a new, concrete historical situation.

In the recent past, more than one theologian dreamed that the Church's doctrine might undergo a new flurry of dogmatic development on varied levels. They foresaw a whole series of specific statements coming in rapid succession. But it may have been only a dream after all, because such a process presupposes that there is a common theology at everyone's disposal.

The cessation of such dogmatic development need not represent an impoverishment of the Church's life of faith or a paralysis of her *sensus fidei*. It only means that the Church would concentrate more fully on the most central issues of the Christian faith, and the present spiritual situation of the world offers much inducement for such concentration. Moreover, these central issues are being examined, interpreted and made real by widely differing theologies.

The interplay of central issues and differing theologies certainly offers as much room for a vital *sensus fidei* as does the older notion of dogmatic development. This older notion, cherished by many theologians in the last few centuries, saw "new dogmas" as the goal and purpose of any development of dogma.

It is also clear that the existing dogmatic statements of the Church will serve a different function than they used to. They will no longer serve as a *terminus a quo* for the development of new dogmas within the framework of a unique theology. Instead, they will serve as the given expression of a common credal profession, to which the many and varied theologies will ultimately relate.

V

But let us look at the problem again. We cannot verify the oneness of our credal profession by pointing to the verbal identity of the credal formulas used. The various theologies use different formulas, and we must respect this variety. Moreover, the pluralism in the theologies which try to explain this credal profession is something which is insurmountable. Now if all this is true, we may have to adopt an entirely different approach in trying to reconcile theological pluralism with credal unity.

Credal Formulas as Signposts

If we want to make progress here, we must first realize certain things. Faith and credal profession, as they are understood in the Church, cannot exist or do without words. For many people, the oneness and sameness of their faith and creed cannot be verified in a wordless context—e.g., an atmosphere of shared feelings, a collaborative effort, or a cultic act (leaving aside the fact that these situations are rarely wordless anyway).

But even these words, as such, have a signpost character. They point to realities, happenings and experiences which are not present to us by virtue of these words alone. Faith and credal profession are not purely and simply "word happenings" that are enclosed within themselves. Human beings need words to communicate and fashion unity among themselves, but the "word happening" alone is not the whole of this unity. The words point toward a unity which they do indeed allow to unfold, but which they do not fashion by themselves alone.

Words themselves, as conceptual abstracts, point toward the mystery of God, the historical reality from which mankind derives, and the world and activities which men share. In short, they point to realities which always involve words but which are not simply identical with the words themselves. These realities are mediated to us by words, but they are experienced as being present, not absent.

Thus, in words we have the possibility of verifying a unity of Word which is not the product of words alone. This possibility presupposes the Christian faith as a given datum, totally independent of the problem posed by comtemporary theological pluralism. How else could one individual be sure of his agreement with another individual in personal convictions, if the other person's convictions can be mediated to him only through his own consciousness? The human mind never verifies this agreement simply by establishing the identical nature of the conceptual content. Real community, identical *utterances* (as opposed to purely abstract thinking) and common concrete action are necessary elements in verifying the sameness of many people's convictions.

The Practice of Unity

In Christendom we find the same baptism performed as a concrete action, and a concrete cultic worship celebrated by all. All our words point to the same historical reality, and to features of it that cannot be explicitated conceptually. Moreover, we all must operate together in the concrete framework of the spatio-temporal world. These facts and many others are not simply the products of a common conviction which we have already verified on the theoretical level. On the contrary, they are elements through which this common conviction is shaped and seen to be real.

The circle has no beginning or end. Common concrete activity (in the broadest sense) is not only the result of a shared conviction; it is also the way in which we fashion this common conviction and come to take cognizance of it. The maintenance and verification of credal oneness amid theological pluralism depends in no small measure (but not entirely) on the fact that this oneness is made real and operative in deeds. In deeds we will find a oneness that can never be provided by concepts alone.

Verification of credal oneness will always remain a human process. It will never be fully achieved once for all time; it will always involve an element of longing and hope. If we wish to achieve credal oneness and to verify it, then we must *utter* this profession together, concretely celebrate the death of the Lord together, execute the sacraments together, and engage in joint activity in the world. Through these activities, the oneness and sameness of our credal profession will become real, whatever pluralism may exist in theology.

VI

ECUMENICAL REPERCUSSIONS

In conclusion, we might well ask what all this will mean for ecumenical theology and the effort to reunite the Christian Churches. Here again, no definitive answer can be offered. We merely offer some reflections.

In the light of what we have already said, we might well ask this question: Is it possible that, unnoticed by us, the theologies of the separated Churches have largely converged into the theological pluralism that should really be found within the one united Church? The reason is not simply that these theologies have undergone further development since the Reformation—a fact alluded to by all. On a deeper level, it is because they now occupy a different place of importance in the credal outlook of their individual Churches. In other words, they now are put at a greater distance from credal profession in every Church, and are viewed in a larger context which leaves room for the legitimate coexistence of many theologies.

In this new context, the theologies of the various Churches may no longer be incompatible to any great extent. Perhaps we can accord them the large measure of autonomous responsibility which we proposed earlier, without requiring a common theological formulation of old or new credal professions as a pre-condition for their coexistence in the one Church. Perhaps there is a real theological possibility, not only of moving from a unified profession of faith to a unified Church, but also of moving from a reunited Church to a unified credal profession or some other satisfactory verification of this unity.

I offer these reflections, but I have no cure-all to prescribe for the credal differences between us. But we must ask ourselves this question: If genuine theological pluralism does exist in the Catholic Church, and has a right to exist, what implications does this have for our ecumenical efforts in the quest for Church unity?

PART II
BIBLIOGRAPHICAL
SURVEY

Langdon Gilkey/*Chicago, Illinois*

Trends in Protestant Apologetics

I

THE PARADOXICAL RELATION OF
PROTESTANT THEOLOGY TO APOLOGETICS

This article on trends in recent Protestant apologetics will attempt to uncover the most significant principles evident in a few recent types of Protestant apologetics with the ultimate aim of drawing some constructive conclusions about apologetics in the near future. We make no pretense, therefore, to provide here an exhaustive or scholarly description of the wide variety of existing Protestant theologies. Protestantism has always exhibited a strange paradoxical—not to say schizophrenic—relation to apologetics. Protestantism can legitimately be described on the one hand as a form of theology which views itself methodologically as wholly *a se,* self-based on religious authorities alone, and thus as not only unconcerned with apologetics of any sort, but also scornful of all who favor such efforts—as the Reformers and certainly Karl Barth well illustrate. Or, on the other hand, Protestant theology has with equal legitimacy been defined as the paradigmatic *Kulturtheologie,* as a form of theology essentially apologetic in structure, in which doctrines arise not at all solely from indigenous religious authorities, but in interaction with, if not subservience to, cultural phenomena. And one thinks first of Schleiermacher's classic definition of Christian theology as in form a philosophical theology that has apologetics as its central task,[1] and secondly of the innumerable re-editions since his time of Protestant theologies based on this philosophy or that, or that understand Christian symbols exhaustively in sociological, psychological, or politico-ethical terms, especially in the United States. Can these two sharply opposing attitudes to apologetics both be *Protestant*? And if so, how is this possible?

Surely any fully defensible answer to this question must take us too far from our topic. Briefly, one may suggest that the essential Protestant note in theology has been a dialectical or polar relation between the direct, absolute and unmediated authority of God through his Word on the one hand, and the personal reception or apprehension of this gift in conscious faith on the other. Thus the Reformers struggled against both ecclesiastical and philosophical mediation of the Word on the one hand— against all mixing of the Word of God with that of man; and yet, on the other, they also argued against the doctrine of implicit faith and the category of unconscious grace, asserting that what God says to man must be vitally affirmed and so intelligibly expressed by every man, and what God does in man must be consciously apprehended by him.[2] The one tendency moves powerfully against every philosophical mediation, every "making intelligible" in ordinary human terms of the biblical categories lest they be contaminated with the idolatries of philosophy.[3]

---

[1] F. Schleiermacher, *Brief Outline of the Study of Theology*, tr. by T. N. Tice (1966), nn. 33, 35, 39, 41. One is also reminded of Tillich's definition of his theology as an "apologetical theology".

[2] "You die by yourself, so you had better believe by yourself": Martin Luther, "First Wittenberg Sermon, 1522," in *Works of Martin Luther* II, p. 391.

[3] Two well-known passages from Calvin represent the Reformation attitude towards "human conceptions" of God: (1) "Whence we may infer that the mind of man is, if I may be allowed the expression, a perpetual factory of idols. . . . The true state of the case is that the mind of man, being full of pride and temerity, dares to conceive of God according to its own standard, and, being sunk in stupidity and immersed in profound ignorance, imagines a vain and ridiculous phantom instead of God": J. Calvin, *The Institutes* I tr. by J. Allen (1936), ch. XI, sec. viii. (2) "For I think we ought to speak of God with the same religious caution, which should govern our thoughts of him: since all the thoughts

And in such a Protestantism the biblical symbols are presented without philosophical interpretation, "as is", in their stark, paradoxical, mythical, uncultural, and yet personal, kerygmatic power —and apologetics remains excluded as a guilty worldling. The other tendency, historically illustrated by Protestant liberalism—that one devoted to the personal experiencing, the intelligible grasping and the voluntary affirming of the faith— moves equally powerfully toward interpreting the bibilical message in contemporary categories so that "the modern man can believe and understand it", and so is in continual danger of losing its transcendent strangeness entirely.

Heretofore, Catholicism has seemed, to me at least, to be more characterized by mediation than by these stark antitheses: on the one hand, the divine authority expressed in the strange biblical categories was mediated by traditional credal and theological formulations; on the other, the requirement of intelligibility in terms of cultural experience was mediated by a traditional (Thomistic) philosophical natural theology and its resultant modes of theological language. My own guess is that in the opaque future Catholicism will inexorably come much closer to this interesting, if mildly insane, Protestant pattern of biblical absoluteness and cultural absorption. As its traditional theological authorities, both credal and philosophical, lose their power in modern life, it will inevitably search, as it seems now to be doing, for both a more unmediated divine authority in Scripture and yet for secularly defensible and credible foundations for its faith. In any case, these introductory remarks may help us to see why Protestant theology has exhibited such a strange set of relations

---

that we entertain concerning him merely from ourselves are foolish and all our expressions absurd. . . . We should seek in the scriptures a certain rule, both for thinking and for speaking, by which we may regulate all the thoughts of our minds, and all the words of our mouths. . . . But what forbids our expressing in plainer words those things which, in the scriptures, are, to our understanding, intricate and obscure, provided our expressions religiously and faithfully convey the true sense of the scriptures, and are used with modest caution, and not without sufficient occasion?": *ibid.*, ch. XIII, sec. iii.

with apologetics. It seems driven almost to self-immolation through a cultural apologetics by its need to be intelligible to and affirmable by the ordinary believer. And yet apologetics also seems to the Protestant mind to be an impossible, not to say treasonous, activity, because in doing apologetics the theologian must use philosophy, he must relate his symbols to ordinary experience, and he must submit to the canons of secular inquiry, so that what he says will be credible and intelligible to the modern world. And if he thus "culturizes" his theological language, asks the Protestant, what then becomes of the absolute Word of God which he must proclaim?

II
The Relations of Neo-Orthodox
Protestant Theology to Apologetics

As is well-known, the recently dominant mode of Protestant theology—which we may call neo-orthodox, neo-Reformation, or biblical theology—represented in almost classical form the first type of Protestant ethos described above. Especially in its Barthian wing, this theology scorned all apologetic efforts as usurpation by human wisdom of the tasks of the Holy Spirit, and it regarded natural theology with unfeigned horror, as one of the more serious forms of blasphemy. It is still hard for any continental Protestant theologian to listen to an argument in natural theology without feeling that he has desecrated some holy place. This antipathy in recent Protestant theology to all argument for the cause of the Gospel, resulting in the extensive search for a common ground with secular experience, is well known. While granting its emotional force on the continent, we should not, however, take this antipathy at face value, since a look at actual practice will reveal powerful apologetic tendencies frequently at work in neo-orthodoxy, and often with magnificent success. To clarify this point, we must distinguish between apologetics and natural theology, for in our view neo-orthodoxy on the whole was powerfully apologetical without practicing any form of natural theology. By apologetics in the widest sense, we mean any consistently argued effort to show the relevance and the meaning (and even in some cases the validity) of the Christian view of things, an effort which for the strength of its argument appeals to some elements of general (as opposed to Christian) experience and so does not depend exhaustively or *in toto* on either revelational authority or the assent of faith. Thus on this definition an apology can be conducted as a prolegomenon or an introduction to faith, showing its relevance, its value, its illuminating power, and so on without attempting or claiming to demonstrate its *truth.* Correspondingly, natural theology is a species within the apologetic genus which seeks and claims to demonstrate on the grounds solely of general experience and rational argumentation, without explicit appeal to any revelational authority, the *validity* of certain doctrines of faith (i.e., that God exists, that the soul is immortal, and so on). It seems to me, then, that neo-orthodoxy as a whole exhibited marked and potent forms of apologetics (in the sense above), while vigorously and correctly denying that it illustrated a natural theology. Barthians were right to accuse Brunner, the Niebuhrs, Tillich, and Bultmann of being "apologists"; they were quite wrong in saying they believed in natural theology.

In what way, then, were the more moderate elements of the neo-orthodox spectrum apologetic? The general principle characteristic of all neo-orthodox theology was the assertion of the radical need of man as finite and sinful for divine grace, both for him to know the truth and for him to do the good. If that need is *total,* of course, then no common human ground between the situation of sin and the coming of grace can be found, and no apologetic is possible or useful. If, however, the man who is in need is the same *man* as he who is given faith, and if (and this is crucial) his "openness" to faith and its viewpoint is a relevant condition to his reception of grace, then apologetics is possible and useful in this framework. What it might do is, in short, to prepare the way for the act of hearing and believing; apologetical argument could, like the law, be a schoolmaster that leads the unbeliever (in church or outside) to Christ. Accordingly, it was generally agreed that argument could accomplish no more than this preparatory work; it could not generate either belief itself or the symbols and doctrines of the faith. What argument could do, then, was to make the given or revealed faith seem relevant and meaningful to man's experienced situation; it could present the viewpoint of faith as a powerful *option* or *possibility* for the man who understands himself correctly. What moved faith from being such a possibility to becoming an actuality was regarded by all as, from the human side, a decision, leap or commitment incommensurate with argument, and, from the divine side, a gift of grace, the work of "grasping" (to use Tillich's language) of the Holy Spirit. It was in this view that most of the leaders of neo-orthodoxy—Brunner, Aulen, Nygren, Bultmann, Tillich and the Niebuhrs—conducted apologetics during the 1930's, 1940's and 1950's.

Given this fundamental theological framework, apologetical argument could, and did, take several important forms. First of all, the error of competing points of view—naturalistic, scientistic, liberal-humanitarian, idealistic, and so on—could be shown. Before 1940, such arguments were less necessary in Europe than in England or America, for in the former a turbulent social history had already destroyed most of these cultural alternatives to faith. Where such secular alternatives remained powerful—as surely in the United States—the writings of Kierkegaard, of Barth (unintentionally?), Brunner and Bultmann, and the arguments of the Niebuhrs, Tillich and their followers, had great apologetic effect in showing to many who as yet had no "faith", especially in the younger generation, the inadequacy of the humanistic alternatives to Christianity and the power of the Christian understanding of man and of history to illuminate what was evidently true about experience. When such arguments were intentional and the apologetics explicit, they were based on historical, social and psychological evidence of various sorts; and what they sought to demonstrate was that neither man's reason nor his virtue was as "pure" as humanists believed them to be, and consequently that the hope or faith of humanism in man's goodness and his capacity autonomously to create meaning was in fact an illusion—whether in his individual life or his social-historical existence.[4] If, therefore (so the argument ran), life is to have meaning and hope—and the liberal culture as well as the Christian culture believed these two were possible and necessary—*then* Christianity provides the only really relevant alternative. On the other hand, they argued that the creativity and the chaos of historical experience, which humanism itself obviously misunderstood and misinterpreted, could be made intelligible through "biblical faith" and its categories of the *imago Dei,* the fall of man and the sovereignty and promises of God. The "common ground", then, on which the argument was conducted was, first, the human situation, personal and histori-cal, which the theologian could interpret in the light of the bibli-cal point of view, and, second, the assumed factor of hope for betterment, or, in theological terms, the evidential character of man's creativity amid his sin and lostness, and the presence even in this situation of the longing for and hope of grace.

A second form of neo-orthodox apologetics found its common ground not in the character of the human situation but in the assumed values of our Western cultural life, values which, it was maintained, owed their existence to the biblical tradition. Thus such essential elements of our cultural "Geist" as the linear view of time, a sense of the meaningfulness of time and especially of history, an affirmation of the value of the material world and the body, an affirmation of the value of the individual and his free-doms, balanced by the concept of a community of persons, and correspondingly democracy, social reform—even an affirmation

[4] Possibly the classical locus for these types of apologetical arguments is R. Niebuhr's *Nature and Destiny of Man* I (1941), pp. 1-150, and *Faith and History* (1949), esp. chs. I, VI, IX, X. Another good example, where the apologetical argument is less explicit, is E. Brunner's *Man in Revolt,* tr. by O. Wyon (1947), pp. 215-478. Cf. also A. Richardson, *Christian Apologetics* (1947) and J. V. Langmead-Casserly, *The Chris-tian in Philosophy* (1949). And for a secondary example, cf. the author's *Maker of Heaven and Earth* (1959).

of sensuality!—were traced to their biblical roots and shown to lodge there. Two implications followed: (1) the Greeks were mostly to blame for the errors in our cultural life—completely reversing the assessment of German classicism and romanticism of the Hellenic and the Hebrew spirits! (2) the biblical tradition *must* (though this argument was left implicit) have revelation as its ultimate source if so much that we now recognize as true and significant comes out of that tradition. Although neo-orthodoxy scorned arguments for faith based on culture and so on the word of man, in these latent appeals to certain firmly held Western attitudes and ideals as in some sense giving ground for belief in biblical revelation, it illustrated covertly what Protestant liberalism had practiced overtly. Such arguments had, of course, a great deal of power (whether they were implicit as in continental writings, or explicit as in Anglo-Saxon theology). That many of these ideas important to our culture's life ultimately had biblical roots is undoubtedly true—but it is also true that they had other roots; [5] and it is even more true that the Church—and thus the Christian tradition—had spent a great deal of her energy combating precisely most of these same concepts. Thus this pattern of apologetics probably tended more to obscure than to reveal our historical past.

Such methods worked well with a generation that (1) was disillusioned with humanism, and with Marxism, and (2) still believed in many of the positive elements of Western culture. Christianity seemed to them a good way—better than Marxism—of combining realism with confidence and thus with an active, moral involvement in Western historical life. The human situation, so interpreted, seemed to establish that transcendence was no meaningless category, that judgment and grace were des-

[5] For example, the Zoroastrian roots of the linear conception of time; the Greek sources for our Western ideals of individuality, community, freedom, justice, order and truth; the Renaissance and Romantic sources for our appreciation of the body and of the sensual life; the Enlightenment sources for our understanding of the need for freedom, autonomy and human well-being in personal, political, social and academic affairs— not to mention the influence of Hegel, Feuerbach, Nietzsche, Marx and Freud in conceiving and developing ideas now embraced as "biblical".

perately needed in human history, and that only the future held grounds for real hope. The authority of the biblical word, the fact of revelation and the presence of the Spirit in the Church seemed intelligible and convincing in the light of the fact that the Christian point of view alone seemed to have illuminating power in a troubled history. Still, this apologetics could not—and did not try to—create "faith". It could at best show the relevance, the meaning—if not the validity—of the Christian symbols. The reason for this hesitancy at the brink or threshold was twofold. (1) The theological symbols (God, revelation, sin, grace and so on) were not induced as hypotheses from the evidence pointed to, from the human situation so described; rather, they were brought already full blown, so to speak, to the evidence to illumine it. Thus they did not function as explanatory hypotheses derived from experience alone, and so they could not be tested in any strictly "empirical" way. They had their origin, as was stated frequently, in biblical faith, in revelation and its reception—and not out of an autonomous, rational analysis of ordinary experience. (2) It was realized on the psychological level that faith was a personal, existential act or decision (here Kierkegaard was very crucial), and on the theological level that faith arose not out of argument, but in the personal response to the encounter with God in the Word, the judgment of the law and the promise of the Gospel.[6] On both grounds—namely, that Christian doctrines arise out of revelation, and that faith arises in response to revelation and the work of the Holy Spirit— apologetics was not confused with natural theology; its work was preparatory and ancillary only.

One remaining aspect of neo-orthodox apologetics arose from

[6] This is especially clear, for example, in Brunner. He uses in his writings all the apologetical arguments described in the text, but insists that "faith" results not from argument but from the Encounter alone. However, he then veers off on another apologetical "tack" and shows that since the secular understanding of the person implies also an I-Thou encounter, Christian faith which has that relation at its center proves itself to be more intelligible and illuminating for personal existence than any other. Cf. E. Brunner, *op. cit.*, and *The Divine-Human Encounter* (1938).

the very close association of neo-orthodox theology to existentialism. While this apologetics recognized that it could *prove* neither the reality of revelation nor the validity of the symbols derived from it, still it was able to extend its apologetics one step further into the area of decision-making. For it could be shown, so they believed, that all men *must* have faith to live, that such faith involves a "mythology" or a system of symbols which cannot be proved, and that thus such faith must come from a decision or stance adopted in life. Thus—they argued—the apologetical issue is not to be drawn between a cool, objective reason on the one hand and faith on the other, or between science and faith, proofs and faith. Rather, in actual existence, the issue lies between various undemonstrable stances adopted in existence on the basis of personal, existential decisions. For the ultimate roots of science itself and of the most objective philosophies lie in unprovable affirmations about reality and truth; or, as Tillich put this point, every philosophy has theological roots. Rational debate in these areas thus concerns not proofs but comparisons of ultimate points of view—all based on faith—and in such a situation Christian faith can show its relative intelligibility and power. Apologetics could not bridge the gulf between a secular stance and a faith stance; but it could show that both were "stances" similar in form, and thus why it was humanly intelligible that the gulf was there, and that this was an inescapable—rather than a puerile—aspect of the human situation.

One of the clearest examples of Protestant apologetics without natural theology was Paul Tillich's correlation theology.[7] Convinced that no doctrine had meaning for man unless it related to the problems and crises of his everyday, cultural or secular existence, Tillich sought to "correlate" the problems of the human situation, as analyzed by his existentialist-ontological philosophy, with the "answers" of revelation, interpreted therefore in the light of that philosophical analysis. Thus was his theology apologetic in its fundamental systematic form. That is, it began with

[7] P. Tillich, *Systematic Theology* I-III (1951), esp. Vol. I, pp. 3-71. Also *The Courage to Be* (1952).

the ordinary situation of man, uncovered a problem latent there which any man might experience, showed that the problem had no solution on the human level, and then demonstrated the relevance and thus the meaning of the theological doctrine related to the problem so interpreted. Our suggestion is that although most neo-orthodox viewed Tillich's method as a capitulation of the Word to culture and philosophy, they in fact followed this method almost point by point: an analysis of the weakness and crises of culture, a demonstration that culture cannot answer these problems, an argument that only Christian categories or doctrines do in fact answer it, and finally an interpretation of the Word in the terms of some compelling and relevant set of secular categories (for example, the use of Heidegger's existentialism in Bultmann, or the use of Buber's concept of the dialogic character of the self as an "I" in relation to a "Thou", explicitly in Brunner and implicitly in most of the other neo-orthodox).

Before we discuss the very serious present difficulties with this mode of apologetics, let us note that many of the general principles uncovered here, with some significant differences to be sure, characterize current and powerful modes of Protestant theology on the continent—for example, that of Gerhard Ebeling and of Jürgen Moltmann. In neither case is a natural theology or a proof of the validity of faith or of any of its symbols entertained. And yet apologetics is embarked upon, if not openly, at least seriously. In the case of Ebeling, the symbols of the law and the Gospel are applied to the general human situation, and to its history, to illumine both; and the category of Word-event (derived from the later Heidegger) is used first to explicate the general human situation ("existence is linguistic") and then its paradigmatic role in the event of faith is shown. In other words, the viewpoint most appropriate for understanding faith in relation to revelation is claimed to be a viewpoint fruitful for understanding all of human existence, and so the whole framework of faith is rendered intelligible and relevant.[8] In Moltmann the parallel

[8] G. Ebeling, *Word and Faith* (1963), esp. chs. II, VI, VIII, XI-XV. Also *The Nature of Faith* (1961), esp. chs. I, VI-XI.

with the older neo-orthodox modes of apologetics is even plainer. Moltmann, too, sees certain categories essential to modern life as arising out of the biblical tradition: the sense of linear time, the sense of the "new" as a possibility in history, and above all the confidence in the future which he labels hope. These, he points out, characterize the modern spirit; hence (so the latent argument runs), if you hold with that spirit, you must recognize the significance and thus the possible validity of the faith from which they arise.[9] Second, if man is to live at all, and *a fortiori* if his world is to become better, and thus if the important secular category of revolution is to be a live possibility—and he believes it is—man must live in a framework which makes it intelligible and plausible to hope.[10] But the only ground for real hope is eschatological. Thus the biblical eschatology is, again, intelligible and plausible as a basis for this human and historical necessity. The logic of the argument parallels the old neo-orthodox patterns: as faith was a necessity against all humanistic alternatives if history is to have meaning, so now hope based on the resurrection is a necessity against all secular alternatives (the bourgeois faith in progress or the Marxist view of the dialectic of history) if revolution is to be possible.

In relating the resurrection as an historical event to this eschatological hope, however, Moltmann and Wolfhart Pannenberg veer off from the neo-orthodox tradition of apologetics we have outlined. Insofar as the claim is made (as it is by both) not only that the Bible witnesses to the resurrection as an historical event, but further that the resurrection so understood can be established as an historical event by the recognized methods of historical inquiry, this is not only apologetics, but even, one might say, a natural theology of the most extreme sort! For it seeks to prove the historical "factuality" of the resurrection as the prior basis of faith instead of its *result* [11] and thus to prove it by the eyes of

[9] J. Moltmann, *The Theology of Hope* (1967), pp. 88, 92f., 106ff., 230f., 261ff. Also "The Category of the New in Christian Theology," in M. Muckenhirn, *The Future as the Presence of Shared Hope* (1968).

[10] Cf. *The Theology of Hope*, pp. 24ff., 64ff., 91ff., 208-12, 269, 284ff.

[11] For Moltmann, cf. *The Theology of Hope*, pp. 172ff. The major

historical reason rather than of faith. Thus are they involved in natural theology—that is, the effort to establish the validity of a claim of faith as well as its relevance and meaning, its possibility.[12] Insofar, however, as they both (and they do) *redefine* the word "history" away from its secular usage among historians (where the category of the miraculous is regarded on various grounds, similar to those enunciated long ago by Hume and more recently by Troeltsch, as *a priori* unavailable to the historian) to a usage appropriate to faith,[13] this enterprise ceases to be either a natural theology or an apologetical effort, and becomes an explication of one of the crucial *results* of looking at an aspect of sacred history through the eyes of faith, and thus

---

theme of the whole of chapter III is that the acceptance of, belief in, and thus knowledge of the resurrection as an objective historical reality precede and are the foundation for our knowledge of God's power, faithfulness and promises, and thus of our faith in God's future—rather than the reverse (namely a belief in the resurrection based on a prior faith). For Pannenberg's view that the reality of the resurrection can and must be established by historical inquiry *prior* to faith, cf. W. Pannenberg, "The Revelation of God in Jesus," in *Theology as History,* ed. by J. M. Robinson and J. B. Cobb, Jr. (1967), pp. 128-29, 131. Also cf. *Jesus: God and Man* (1968), pp. 27-28, 88-92, 97-99.

[12] For a deeply critical discussion of supposedly "historical" arguments on behalf of the resurrection, when in reality faith alone makes these arguments plausible, cf. V. Harvey, *The Historian and the Believer* (1966), esp. pp. 104-10.

[13] For Moltmann, cf. *The Theology of Hope,* pp. 173-74, 180-81, 190. As he says: "The [modern] experience of history is confronted also by a different [Christian or post-resurrection] experience of history" (p. 175). What else is this but to presuppose *faith* as the ground of the acceptance of the resurrection as a possibility? For Pannenberg, cf. *Jesus: God and Man,* p. 97: "Certainly the possibilities that he can consider in this will depend upon the understanding of reality that he brings with him to his task. If the historian approaches his work with the conviction that the dead do not rise, then it has already been decided that Jesus also has not risen." But, we must ask, for a theology which eschews a natural theology, what *can* be the basis of the historian's denial that "the dead do not rise"—i.e., his belief in the possibility of a resurrection, *except* faith. Certainly it can be neither reason nor experience! To emphasize the "tradition" of such an expectation is simply to find a new sociological and historical way of describing faith, which relates us to such a tradition. In any case, no one but a believer would find the "historical" arguments which Pannenberg offers (pp. 88-106) for the reality of the resurrection anything but extremely shaky and unsound.

through eyes that take for granted the possibility of such an event in history. In the first case, the "common ground" of historiography is appealed to; in the second case, an acknowledgment of the Word of God in Scripture and thus the possibility of divinely instituted events are assumed as the conditions for understanding the events reported in the New Testament—and so here there is no common ground at all. It seems evident to this observer that whatever the fruitfulness of the "neo-orthodox style" apologetic of Moltmann vis-à-vis the categories of the new and of revolution, there is in our age no possibility of answering the questions of fundamental doubt (which *is* the apologetic task)—either that of the Christian or that of the unbeliever—through an appeal to biblical authority on the one hand and to the factuality of a resurrection on the other. Both the assent to biblical authority and the conviction that a resurrection is credible as an historical, factual event, presuppose Christian faith and thus precisely exclude the sort of doubt to which apologetical argument is *ipso facto* addressed. Thus we do not find this new trend in Protestant apologetics to be a very promising departure from the sort of apologetics Protestant theology has offered for some time.

Practical Difficulties

What, then, are the difficulties presently characteristic of the general mode of neo-orthodox apologetics we have described? First, it should be said that, at least in American circles, it is considered for the present to have lost its persuasive power. Few try to "do" theological apologetics in that way anymore. Thus, even aside from the appeal to the resurrection, it is this which makes current continental Protestant theology, however brilliant in its biblical and historical scholarship, seem anachronistic to us. Why is this so? In general one can say that the basic presuppositions of this mode of apologetics have themselves recently been so radically questioned that an apologetics that makes these assumptions seems to beg rather than to answer the questions to which contemporary apologetics should address itself. As we recall, the fundamental form of this apologetics was roughly as follows: *if* life, history and the paradoxes of human existence are to become intelligible, have meaning and be transformed, *then* the Christian symbols, derived from revelation, provide the necessary framework within which meaning, intelligibility and even transformation are to be achieved. Three problems arose in the intervening years with regard to these presuppositions of neo-orthodox apologetics.

(1) First of all, the apologetics appealed to the necessity of an ultimate framework of meaning if men are to live creatively and actively toward hte future: if life is to have meaning, then. . . . Now, in any if-then proposition, radical doubt about the "if" renders the "then" irrelevant. Thus serious doubt about the possibility of the meaningfulness of "an ultimate framework of meaning" —be it providential, christological or eschatological—certainly cuts down on the apologetical value of this approach. Here existentialism, linguistic philosophy and the problem of evil—ironically, aids earlier in the growth of neo-orthodoxy—signaled its destruction. In its most extreme forms, existentialism questioned whether an "ultimate framework of meaning" was not a hindrance rather than a help to man's authenticity.[14] Linguistic philosophy in turn asked whether words about the "meaning of history", the "new in history" and so on had themselves any meaning at all, and, if so, what sorts of meaning. Finally, it has been asked whether, far from giving a framework of *meaning* to history's turmoil, the belief in the sovereignty of the covenant God does not, in the light of present evil, make impossible, or at any rate immoral, any kind of historical meaning.[15] In sum, in the present rather skeptical philosophical and quite desperate historical situation, the argument that the framework of faith gives "meaning" to historical life seems to be subverted by the challenge that to the secular mentality the framework of faith itself has little meaning and less plausibility and thus is hardly convincing as a basis

---

[14] Cf., in this regard, A. Camus, *The Rebel* and *The Plague;* J.-P. Sartre, *Being and Nothingness.*

[15] R. Rubenstein, *After Auschwitz* (1966), esp. chs. 2-8.

for either meaningfulness or hope. And it is surely obvious that such modern and very secular questions about the existential, the linguistic and the moral implications of "ultimate frameworks of historical meaning" in general and that of faith in particular are not answered by appeals to the characteristic affirmations and doctrines of the Bible itself. It is no answer to the question of the plausibility of the fundamental viewpoint of the Bible to point out that according to that view such doubt is to be expected, that for the Bible meaning is illusive, evil frequently rampant, God hidden and doubt often an aspect of genuine faith. Biblical faith *is* characterized in part by doubt. But that is not a convertible proposition. Doubt is not necessarily identical with biblical faith, and it is useless to pretend it is or that serious doubt is not a threat to faith as well as an element of it. There are levels of doubt that exclude faith, and that thus cannot be answered by repeating again the implications of the contents of faith.

(2) The neo-orthodox apologetics assumed the presence, so to speak, in the hands of the theologian of a set of meaningful and illuminating biblical categories. These he had not induced from his analysis of secular experience; rather, he found them in biblical revelation, and then in his own apologetic work he applied them to secular experience to illumine it. Their intrinsic meaningfulness and validity thus depended entirely on divine revelation and on the communal and personal or historical faith that "knew" man as sinner, God as Lord, Christ as risen, or the future as hope; it was *faith,* in relation to the Word, that knew these things, and then applied them to personal and historical experience to illumine and clarify the ambiguities there. The *cognitive* base of theology here was thus faith in response to the Word; if that slipped, then the whole logical structure of biblical theology and the potency of its apologetical forms would slip, too. The difficulty has been that it *has* slipped. Perhaps it should not have done so—perhaps doubt at this level indicates one is no longer a Christian. Be that as it may, many laymen, pastors and theological students have experienced doubt at this level—

namely, a gnawing doubt whether they in fact *had* faith or not, whether they had received revelation at all, whether they really *knew* these things the biblical language talked about, and whether, consequently, these symbols about God and his acts which they applied to experience *meant* anything to them even when they proclaimed them. What had happened was this. (1) They experienced in themselves secular doubt eroding their confidence in the reality of faith as a qualification of their *own* existence, thus eroding in turn their sense of the meaning, the validity and the certainty of the doctrines of faith. Even if, for example, it were undeniable that "faith *knows*" the Lord as risen, they were not sure that they themselves *had* that sort of faith and that they personally knew that as truth. (2) As a consequence, it had finally to be admitted that the theologian, the pastor and the layman were themselves qualified as much by "secularity" as by "faith", that their apprehension of reality and thus their standards of validity and meaning were as much, if not more, secular than Christian. Thus "Church" and "world" were not two positions (as neo-orthodoxy had viewed them), but *one:* the Church was wordly and thus saturated by worldly doubt as much as by churchly faith. The radical or "God is dead" theology expressed powerfully for many this situation.[16] For many who did not agree with the theological conclusions of this school, it nevertheless brought to consciousness this intermixture in Christian existence, in our time of difficulties and doubts with our faith arising from our secularity, that for us belief is also characterized by unbelief.

A further consequence of this development was that the questions determining apologetics shifted. The essential and prior question seemed to be not merely, how a theological viewpoint illumines the secular situation; rather, the question became how a secular man begins to find meaning and validity in theological

[16] Cf. especially W. Hamilton, *The New Essence of Christianity* (1961) and with T. Altizer, *Radical Theology and the Death of God* (1966); T. Altizer, *The Gospel of Christian Atheism* (1966); P. Van Buren, *The Secular Meaning of the Gospel* (1963).

categories. How, starting with secularity and not with faith, can one begin to do theology? If one asks these questions—and these are, I believe, the fundamental questions of present churchmen—then one cannot appeal solely either to revelation or to faith to give meaning and relevance to theology. If the man who hears theology and preaching, in church or out, is himself a secular man in most of his fundamental attitudes toward reality and truth—as we *are*—then theology cannot *start,* as neo-orthodoxy did, with the non-secular assumptions of revelation, the authority of Scripture, the kerygmatic encounter with Christ or the reality of the event of faith, if one is to be intelligible and meaningful. Accordingly, in apologetics we cannot assume the biblical faith and then move from there to secularity as the apologetics of biblical theology did. In the modern situation— certainly in America and in all probability on the continent, too—the task of doing theology is set within a vastly secular atmosphere, an atmosphere which penetrates Church and world alike, belief as well as unbelief, and which makes arduous, though *not* impossible, the credibility and meaning of the symbols of faith. In such a situation we cannot assume the older confessional or biblical authorities, for it is *these* that our secularity, whether we wish it or not, finds itself doubting or at least questioning, and so it is questions about *them* that our own secularity poses for our faith. Thus apologetics is (1) necessary because even faithful churchmen doubt the most fundamental things about the faith, and (2) difficult because older neo-orthodox patterns of apologetics are no longer available to us.

III

APOLOGETICAL TRENDS IN ANGLO-SAXON LIBERAL THEOLOGY

The other major type of Protestant apologetics, characteristic of Anglo-Saxon and not of continental theology, is liberal rather than neo-orthodox in form, for it explicitly uses some form of philosophy as a point of mediation between faith and its doctrines and a modern or secular viewpoint.[17]

The Apologetics of Process-Theology

There are two important wings at present of this type of philosophical theology or religious philosophy. The first is the tradition of process theology, based on the metaphysical philosophy of A. N. Whitehead, and elaborated in various directions by the philosophers H. N. Wieman and Charles Hartshorne. The major present representatives of this school are B. M. Meland, D. D. Williams, John H. Cobb, Jr. and Schubert M. Ogden.[18] For

[17] The form of philosophical theology described here is to be distinguished from the use of Heidegger on the continent—either in Bultmannian terms or in the newer uses of the later Heidegger. On the continent philosophy is used (if at all) to interpret in modern language the event of divine revelation and its contents. Thus God, revelation, the sacral character of the Christ-event, the authority of the apostolic kerygma, and the unique and sacral character of the rise of faith are all *assumed* ab initio; they neither are established by philosophy nor are they themselves subjected to philosophical criticism and so translated into philosophical terms. Rather, philosophy is used to interpret this given and prior theological framework of God, revelation, incarnation and Word-event, which therefore remain intact and untranslated. Philosophy interprets; it does not criticize, translate and so transform the basic structures of this traditional "Word of God" theology. In striking contrast to this, in the philosophical-theological tradition we here describe, no theological categories are given or presupposed *ab initio,* and so *every* theological category is subjected to philosophical criticism, reinterpretation and translation; therefore, it is fair to say that no genuine category of revelation appears here as prior to and foundational for theology. Only those theological categories harmonious with the criteria and requirements of the philosophical scheme are allowed—a vastly different matter from the use which Bultmann, Ebeling or Ott have made of Heidegger, or even that Thomas made of Aristotle! In this discussion of apologetics by means of philosophical mediation, we shall omit one tradition which also has used philosophy exhaustively to criticize, translate and thus to transform theological categories—namely, the idealistic tradition represented in the 20th century, among others, by A. Pringle-Pattison in *The Idea of God in the Light of Recent Philosophy* (1920), and W. Hocking in *The Meaning of God in Human Experience* (1912). We do this largely because idealistic arguments have in recent times been so totally out of both philosophical and theological fashion.

[18] A. Whitehead, *Science and the Modern World* (1925); *Process and Reality* (1927); *Religion in the Making* (1926); H. Wieman, *The Wrestle*

them, as for the liberal tradition of which they are a part, the main task of theology is apologetics—namely the task of making the traditional beliefs and symbols of faith intelligible to the modern mind and thus exhibiting in modern terms their truth. To perform this task, they believe that the categories of traditional faith must be "translated" into a modern metaphysics expressive of (1) modern man's apprehension of things, and yet (2) such that it is compatible with, and thus not destructive of, a "Christian apprehension of things". To them process metaphysics amply fits both roles: it is modern and thus intelligible in terms of modern science, modern standards of empiricism, modern ethical and aesthetic judgments, and so on; and yet, they say, its characteristic contours fit it admirably to be a vehicle of Christian meaning. For example, for process thought God is essentially related rather than unrelated to the world; he is dynamic rather than static in character; he "feels" and directs the world; he is the source of its values without being an arbitrary ruler or tyrant; he persuades rather than determines the world's course. Thus, so they argue, in the terms of this metaphysics such biblical notions as the dynamic activity of God in history, his loving care for the world, his openness for the future as the locus of salvation, the reality of man's freedom and historicity, and so on, are expressed far more intelligibly than by the traditional absolutistic Aristotelian-Thomistic categories which saw God as a transcendent, separated, changeless, and thus unrelated being. Above all, they feel that only if the "myths" of biblical faith are thus exhaustively [19] translated into a coherent, unified metaphysical

_____

of Religion with Truth (1925); Religious Experience and the Scientific Method (1926); The Source of Human Good (1946); C. Hartshorne, Beyond Humanism (1937); Man's Vision of God (1941); The Divine Relativity (1948); The Logic of Perfection (1962); B. Meland, Faith and Culture (1953); The Realities of Faith (1962); The Secularization of Modern Culture (1966); D. Williams, God's Grace and Man's Hope (1949); J. Cobb, Jr., A Christian Natural Theology (1965); The Structure of Christian Existence (1967); S. Ogden, Christ without Myth (1961); The Reailty of God (1966).

[19] It is at this point that this tradition breaks sharply with the con-

language can that faith have persuasive power or religious relevance to modern minds. A metaphysical apologetic, not to say a natural theology, is necessary if Christianity is to remain a live option today. Strangely, therefore, while the *material* contents of this view are violently anti-Thomistic, its *formal* characteristics remind one very much of familiar Thomist structures, in which a "secular" philosophical epistemology and ontology provide the intelligible framework within which the doctrines of the faith are expressed.

The present difficulties of this form of Protestant apologetic, as is also the case with its Catholic Thomistic half-brother, stem more from philosophical than from religious or theological criticism. To be sure, the neo-orthodox outcry against philosophical theology and natural theology alike as destructive of faith still has vast influence on most of those who wish to do theology exclusively from a biblical perspective. Nevertheless, with the weakening in the last years of biblical theology itself, the main difficulties have come from the widespread *philosophical* criticism of metaphysical speculation. The essence of this theology's argument is that only a metaphysical interpretation of religious categories will give meaning and validity to these categories for a modern man. If, therefore, real questions are raised about the intelligibility and meaning for modernity of metaphysics itself, then this theology is left, so to speak, with two sets of dubious language games instead of one. But it is precisely the central characteristic of the most significant forms of contemporary phi-

---

tinental usage of philosophy as noted in footnote 17. In continental theology, say the process theologians, the translation out of mythological categories and into categories intelligible to modern men is not exhaustive or total. God remains uninterpreted by existentialist philosophy. His unique Word to us in Christ, in Scripture and in proclamation—the Word-event—remains unmediated and unrationalized by higher philosophical or metaphysical categories. Thus at its center this theology retains a level of "mythical" discourse about the divine "activity", the divine "coming", "speaking", "judging" and "loving" which are unintelligible to modern men. "Set it *all* in metaphysical categories, or give up talking about demythologization!" Cf. S. Ogden, *Christ without Myth*, especially chs. III and IV.

losophy—at least in Anglo-Saxon life—to question radically the
possibility of metaphysics.

Apologetics Based on Language Philosophy and Their Difficulties

The dominant form of philosophy in England and America is
what is usually called "language philosophy", whether of a positivistic or of an "ordinary language" variety (roughly the "earlier" as opposed to the "later" Wittgenstein). And the essential
note of this philosophy is the abdication of the role of philosophy
as the "knower" of the real and the ultimate, and its consequent,
more modest role as the analyzer of the forms of man's
language.[20] Philosophy does not help us to know the real, "what
is the case". It rather tells us the forms of our discourse; it analyzes propositions made on other grounds (scientific, common
sense, ethical, religious, etc.); it makes no assertions about reality on its own; it reminds us of the *usages* of our words; it does
not tell us to what in "objective reality" they might refer. Thus
metaphysics, whatever else it may be, is hardly a legitimate
branch of philosophical inquiry, and *a fortiori* a natural theology
becomes impossible. On different grounds, but with somewhat
the same effect, existentialism, phenomenology and empirical
naturalism, other important contemporary forms of philosophy,
have also called in question the possibility of speculative metaphysics. Philosophers seem, in other words, to find metaphysical
discourse as "queer" and as empty as they do theological discourse. Consequently, it appears to serve the task of apologetics
little if we translate the one into the other. If the point of theological reflection is to set religious thought into the terms of
modern philosophy, then a metaphysically-based theology seems,
considering the anti-metaphysical character of modern philosophy, to be the option least fruitful for our day.

As a result of some of these factors, the most creative of the

[20] For clear explications of linguistic philosophy, cf. J. Urmson, *Philosophical Analysis* (1956); G. Warnock, *English Philosophy since 1900*
(1958); A. Ayer *et al., The Revolution in Philosophy* (1957); R. Rorty,
The Linguistic Turn (1967); J. Macquarrie in this volume.

theologians in this school have been shifting their emphases away from metaphysical construction as the basis of their apologetics to linguistic or phenomenological analysis. The best example, I believe, is Schubert Odgen. Whereas a few years ago he was calling unambiguously for the translation of religious categories into the terms of a "neo-classical metaphysical system" as an apologetic device, now his apologetical arguments take a very different form.[21] By analyzing the unconscious presuppositions of moral activity and intellectual inquiry alike, Odgen finds implicit in both an affirmation of an ultimate order in existence which is equivalent to faith in God. On the basis, therefore, of the (to him) undeniable truth that man in fact believes in God, statements about God are intelligible and meaningful, and discourse about God can be rationally defended. Such a "phenomenological" analysis of the presuppositions of all affirmations and all affirmative statements is, clearly, not the same as the construction of a metaphysical system; it is rather a phenomenological prolegomenon to metaphysics itself as much as it is to theology, morals and science. As the contemporary problematical character of faith has driven neo-orthodox apologetics off its traditional ground onto new territory, so the parallel problematic of metaphysics has driven philosophical theology to a phenomenological analysis of immediate experience to uncover the grounds alike of philosophy and of religious statements.

The second wing of recent philosophical apologetics in theology has been that which has used not process metaphysics but linguistic or analytical philosophy as its intellectual base. There were few possibilities for Christian apologetics afforded by positivism.[22] However, later "ordinary language philosophy", stemming from the more tolerant approach to modes of language of the later Wittgenstein,[23] opened the door to a wide variety of

[21] Cf. especially the recent title essay in *The Reality of God* (1965).
[22] For one theological use of positivism, cf. W. Zuurdeeg, *An Analytical Philosophy of Religion* (1958).
[23] Cf. especially L. Wittgenstein, *Philosophical Investigations*, tr. by G. Anscomb (1963). For a clarifying discussion of the distinction between the "earlier" and the "later" Wittgenstein, cf. Warnock, *op. cit.*, chs. 9-11, and Urmson, *op. cit.*, chs. 6-7.

such philosophical defenses of religious language in general and of Christian language in particular. As will become clear, such defenses were a form of apologetics and not of natural theology, since they tried to show the meaningfulness and legitimacy of religious language rather than the validity of any particular statements in that language—i.e., that it may be intelligible and meaningful to say "God is" as opposed to proving *that* he is. As we have noted, the main tenet of linguistic philosophy has been that the role of philosophy is not that of a mode of knowing reality, however the latter may be defined. Thus philosophical inquiry does not initiate, test or verify inductive statements about "what is the case"; no philosopher can say on philosophical grounds that God is, or what he is. Rather, the role of philosophy is that of analyzing our various types of language, showing how the words are used, what sorts of criteria for correct and incorrect usage there are, and therefore the kinds of statements in that "language game" that make sense and the kinds that do not. Philosophy is "talk about talk", and its aim is that through inquiry into our confusing linguistic habits it may become a therapist or a healer of the worst of them. If a language game is given—that is, has usage in a community of discourse—the linguistic analyst of this sort can assume that it is intelligible or meaningful, and thus he proceeds through his analysis to find out what sort of intelligibility or "grammar" that language in fact possesses. He does not bring any prior criterion of sense or nonsense to his analysis; all he does is "look and see" what usages there are.[24] In the case of religious language, then, the philosopher's role is to argue neither for it nor against it; assuming that it is "there"—and it seems to be there in the Christian community —his role is to analyze it and show what its grammar is, how it uses words, how it validates or tests its statements, and thus what sort of meaning it in fact has. If an intelligible, although to be sure "queer" or unique, grammar is found to be present in reli-

[24] L. Wittgenstein, *op. cit.*, n. 66, p. 31e; cf. also n. 340, p. 109e, and n. 578, p. 152e.

gious language, then presumably such usage of language, freed from linguistic philosophical attack, has shown itself to be fully meaningful and so defensible. Archbishop Ian Ramsay, I. A. Crombie, Ninian Smart, John Hick, C. H. Hare, Donald Evans and many others have illustrated brilliantly this role of philosophical apologetics.[25]

There are, however, several factors in the current religious and theological situation which raise the question whether this is as useful a mode of apologetics as it at first might seem. As we have noted, ordinary language philosophy must assume that a given language game is in fact given—that is, actually used in a community—in order for its analysis to start. It assumes, therefore, the intelligibility of this usage—i.e., the fact that this language communicates among its users, as a basis for its analysis; and what its analysis does is to exhibit that given intelligibility or communicability of meanings in philosophical, reflective, and thus logical form. Such an analysis, therefore, is not at all equipped to establish or to demonstrate that intelligibility, to recommend religious language as essential to life, to show a secular doubter why this language game should be used in the first place. Nor, correspondingly, is it able to show the meaningfulness of religious symbols to people who wonder if they have any meaning at all—for it must assume that this meaning is there, latent in active usage in a community.

It seems evident, however, that these are the problems which modern apologetics must answer. For the theological problem is *not* that religious language, while used meaningfully in church, is unintelligible to the secular world outside; rather it is that the meaning of this language, as well as its validity, is problematic precisely in the Church: to laymen, clerics, students and theologians alike. For this language game, while "officially" used in

[25] I. Ramsey, *Religious Language* (1957); *Freedom and Immortality* (1960); *Models and Mystery* (1964); *Christian Discourse* (1965); J. Hick, *Faith and Knowledge* (1957); *Philosophy of Religion* (1963); *Evil and the God of Love* (1966). Especially helpful are the essays by Crombie, Smart, Hare and others in the seminal volume edited by A. Flew and A. MacIntyre, *New Essays in Philosophical Theology* (1955).

sermons, prayers, and so on, barely communicates throughout the Church community, is understood by only a few in the Church herself, and is only rarely *used* by any of the Church's people to understand and to communicate about their ordinary life. The problem is that the logical condition necessary for language analysis is not here fulfilled: this language game is *not* in actual use, it is not in fact "given". On the contrary, the apologetical problem—in and to the Church—is precisely that of attempting to show, if that be possible, that a Christian language, at present relatively unintelligible in Church life, can become anew or again intelligible and meaningful to the modern man (so that proclamatory and liturgical speech can mean something to the Church that hears it). And in turn this requires that one exhibit why this language is relevant to, meaningful in, and in fact essential for the ordinary secular milieu in which we all exist. The apologetical problem is that of showing how religious and thus theological discourse is a necessary aspect of our human symbolic life, and what Church language *means* in relation to ordinary, secular experience. Only then can the language of the Church regain the usefulness it has tended to lose in a secular age. But such a relating of a barely used and so actually almost meaningless language game to the manifold of experience is not the function of ordinary language philosophy, which must assume that Church language is actually used in order to begin its apologetical task.[26] Thus linguistic philosophy had to make the same assumptions that neo-orthodox apologetics made—that people in the Church *had* a seamless faith, that therefore they found religious symbols quite intelligible, and consequently that they *used* religious discourse meaningfully. And so, being based

[26] These remarks should not be taken as a blanket negation of all possible uses of linguistic analysis in contemporary apologetics, but rather as a question about its dominant uses in the past. S. Toulmin's discussion of "limiting questions" in *The Place of Reason in Ethics* (1964), ch. 14, and recently D. High's *Language, Persons and Belief* (1967), illustrate other, much more creative uses of language analysis. In each case the relevance of religious forms of discourse to *secular* life is exhibited.

on the same questionable assumptions, this mode of apologetics has tended to weaken during the same period that neo-orthodoxy declined.[27]

IV
WHERE WE SHOULD BE GOING

Since our remarks seem to have left us deep within an intractable dilemma, we might well wonder how in this situation any sort of theology, and *a fortiori* any sort of apologetics, might be possible. In a descriptive article, a constructive elaboration of a new mode of apologetical theology is, of course, impossible. But we might summarize our own feelings of "where we should be going" in these matters in a few brief theses.[28]

(1) If the situation of the Christian in a secular culture is that of a "secular Christian", a religious existence characterized by a secular apprehension of self and reality as well as by a religious or Christian apprehension, and thus an existence qualified by doubt as well as by faith, then for the Church as well as the world the problem of the meaningfulness and the validity of Christian symbols and doctrines, the problem of "faith", is a real

[27] A particularly instructive example of the parallel decline of biblical theology and this mode of apologetics is provided by the work of D. Evans. In an earlier and brilliant book, *The Logic of Self-Involvement* (1963), Evans applied the methods of linguistic analysis (especially that of J. Austin) to an essentially Barthian theological position. That is, he analyzed the "language of biblical faith", especially with regard to creation, to show the grammar and usage latent in biblical statements about God. So long as such biblical faith provided for him a sure, coherent and tenable starting point, raising *in itself* no fundamental theological problems, such a method was useful. However, once the meaning of the biblical statements about God became itself a serious problem, then such a method, which must assume *ab initio* this meaning, becomes impossible. Consequently Evans has himself abandoned this mode of apologetics and embarked, in his latest writings and addresses, on a more phenomenological approach, deriving religious speech from the experiences of grace in Christian life.

[28] A fuller explication and defense of these suggestions is to be found in a forthcoming book *The Renewal of God-Language* (1969).

problem. This means that this problem of meaninglessness or doubt within the Church is one with which theology must deal if theology is to be a Church as well as an academic discipline, an enterprise useful to the life of the Church. It follows, therefore, that dogmatic theology, the theology with which the Church addresses herself, must direct itself to the reality of doubt as well as to the reality of faith. Thus the classical distinction between a confessional or dogmatic theology that assumes faith in revelation and thus in biblical authority on the one hand, and apologetical theology, addressed to unbelief on the other, breaks down. The theology with which the Church addresses herself must be both confessional and apologetic, and so any relevant *dogmatic* theology must have an apologetical element. In this sense the classical liberal and the traditional Catholic insistence on apologetics was correct against the Reformation and Barthian repudiation of them.

(2) While in this situation apologetical theology is a necessity, nevertheless the same situation makes it also extremely difficult. For the spiritual side of modernity, which creates the contemporary need for apologetical theology, is precisely what makes any successful apology seemingly impossible. An apologetical theology addressed to the secular mind (which characterizes the Church in our age as the "Hellenistic mind" characterized the experience and thought of the early Church) can assume *as its starting point* neither the reality of revelation and thus of the authority of Scripture (as did neo-orthodoxy), nor the possibility of metaphysical speculation (as do traditional Catholic and present-day process forms of philosophical theology). Somehow apologetical theology must start from (a) the immediacy of experience rather than the metaphysical analysis of experience, and (b) the immediacy of ordinary, *secular* experience (experience in its general and purely human scope) as opposed to special "faith" experience—for this is where we and our people, insofar as we raise these questions and doubts, *are*.

(3) Consequently, an apologetics that begins with secular

immediacy can only have the form of a prolegomenon to Christian theology. It cannot be in the form of a natural theology, since the ability of reason to uncover by metaphysical inquiry the ultimate structure of the real cannot be presupposed. If philosophical analysis of secular immediacy cannot be assumed even to reach the real, *a fortiori* it cannot be presumed to be able to establish that that real has a Christian form, that the God of Christian faith can be proved. Secondly, while secularity does qualify our existence and thus our reflection, nevertheless it is also true that "faith" is a different stance from that of secularity, a stance which can include what is valid in the secular spirit, but surely does not agree with *all* that that spirit implies. (Again the parallel with the situation of theology in the Hellenistic environment comes to mind.) Thus the symbolic thematization of life characteristic of faith is a special kind of understanding of life, a unique mode of apprehending world, history and self resulting from a special stance and a special mode of experience. Therefore, no analysis of secular immediacy can arrive by a process of argument alone at the stance of faith; rational argument or natural theology cannot establish or directly found Christian theological discourse. It can only be a preparation, a prolegomenon to theological language. In this sense the neo-orthodox were correct against both traditional Catholic and traditional liberal reliance on natural theology.

(4) The role of apologetics as prolegomenon is then not to prove the validity of Christian symbols, but to establish the *meaningfulness* of religious language in general. A phenomenological analysis (or hermeneutic) of ordinary experience can be conducted which will uncover those dimensions of ordinary experience which require religious symbolization if they are to be comprehended at all. It is as thematizations of these dimensions of experience that religious symbols in general and Christian symbols in particular "mean"—here is where they fit into ordinary secular experience; this is their content, that in experience to which they refer. Each cluster or system of religious symbols

(i.e., each religion) itself comes from the particularity of a particular religious tradition and the stance it embodies. For one within that tradition and thus that stance, this particularity and the origin of these symbols are understood in terms of some equivalent to the category of revelation. But religious symbols, including Christian ones, "mean"—i.e., they thematize—our ordinary common experiences of contingency, relativity, autonomy, guilt and transience; fate, sin and death are what the Gospel is "about", and yet they are surely, as much as air, light and bread, a part of ordinary secular experience. To uncover these religious dimensions of secular experience, then, is the role of a prolegomenon. The prolegomenon is apologetical insofar as it shows the reference points in ordinary experience for religious symbols or categories, and thus insofar as it shows the importance and significance of those symbols—their potentiality for validity, so to speak. The prolegomenon is in turn an essential aspect of dogmatic theology insofar as the experiential, if not the eidetic, meaning of the theological symbols, expressive of the faith of the Christian community, is derived and established here.

Clearly such an apologetics as a prolegomenon to theology, rather than as a natural theology—a specifying of the conditions in ordinary experience for the meaningfulness and thus the potential validity of religious and Christian symbols—is much closer to the sort of apologetical trend represented by Karl Rahner than it is to either a classical natural theology or a traditional biblical theology.[29] Like the natural theologian, it agrees with the requirement of a secular analysis as a pre-condition for understanding the meaning of Christian affirmation; but, like the

[29] Reference is here made to *Hörer des Wortes* (1963), since this work embodies an anthropological analysis which delineates man as essentially "listener for the Word"—that is, as an inescapably religious being whose existence is qualified by a religious dimension. The apologetic, however, does not seek to go further and to specify in advance, through its anthropological analysis, the character of the revelation for which man listens. Actually, Rahner for my taste derives far too much of the character of the revealing God and of his message from his prior anthropological analysis!

revelationist, it recognizes that both the eidetic structure of Christian symbols on the one hand, and the affirmation of their validity on the other, are dependent on revelation, the first appearing out of the special events in which the religion is founded, and the second arising only from the experience of faith within the historic community.

John Macquarrie/*New York, New York*

Religious Language and Recent Analytical Philosophy

I

CRITERIA OF EARLY ANALYTICAL PHILOSOPHY

What is the nature of religious language, and what does such language mean? Twenty-five years ago, the typical analytical philosopher would have had a brusque answer to these questions. Such language, he would have told us, is strictly nonsense. It conveys no information about the world or any reality.

Information and Emotion

Not only religious language, but also the languages of morals and metaphysics were denied any cognitive character. Their function was simply to evince emotion. To say "God is love" is not—so the theory ran—to give some information about some mysterious entity called "God"; rather, it is just a complicated way of giving voice to a feeling of security or happiness. One might as well say, "Hurrah". Similarly, to say "Violence is wrong" is not to ascribe some mysterious quality of "wrongness" to violent deeds; it is just to evince a feeling of disapproval with regard to such deeds, so that one might as well say: "Violence! Ugh!"

Some people were quick to point out that the distinction between informative and emotive language is greatly oversimplified. Our feelings are not just free-floating subjective emotions. If

I have a feeling of well-being, it is because I think there are reasons for entertaining such a feeling. If I have a feeling of disapproval with regard to violent deeds, it is because I think that such deeds are worthy of disapproval. Probably there is a good deal of "mixed" language—i.e., language which both conveys information and is a report on the feelings of the speaker.

Verification Principle

However, the reasons for the anaylsts' critique of religious language could be very clearly stated and demand careful consideration. The philosopher points out that statements about what God is doing or about the wrongness of certain kinds of behavior seem to lack any empirical basis. Churchmen frequently make speeches about "what God is doing in the world". Can any meaning be assigned to their words? If someone talks about what President Nixon is doing in the world, I can understand him and also judge whether his statement is true or false. President Nixon is an identifiable person; he gets things done by an identifiable chain of command centered in Washington; from press, radio and television and sometimes even by direct observation, I can find out what he is doing at any given moment. But the matter is entirely different with God. Neither he nor his agents nor his deeds are directly observable, and my suspicions can hardly fail to be aroused when I notice that what he is allegedly doing in the world usually corresponds very closely to the desires of the person who uses such language.

The analyst who is of a positivistic turn of mind (the so-called "logical positivist") sees that there are clear ways of establishing the meaning and truth-value of assertions about President Nixon, for these are open to some kind of empirical verification. But no empirical verification seems relevant to "God is love" or "Violence is wrong", and so one must at least exclude these from statements of fact, though no doubt the positivist was going too far when he concluded that they must therefore be nonsense.

But whatever the excesses of the positivist may have been, at least he did try to give a clear account of the logic of empirical discourse, including the language of the empirical sciences, and he showed that neither moral judgments nor theological assertions belong to the category of empirical language. We often hear it said nowadays that logical positivism is dead, but James Alfred Martin is correct in insisting that the essential challenge of the positivist remains. The positivist has shown the ends and the methods of the language of science, and how this language differs from other kinds of language. "Can the theologian articulate comparable ends?" asks Martin. "How does the God of whom he speaks relate to a world in which there can be the 'joy of cognition'? If he claims to have cognition of God, is it similar to, in conflict with, or compatible with, scientific cognition? The logical positivist makes a *moral* demand of the theologian: that he try to be as clear about what he is and is not saying, and how he goes about justifying his statements, as the scientist and his positivist interpreters are. The demand cannot be responsibly evaded, yet many theologians have sought to evade it by speaking too easily and too soon about the 'disguised metaphysics' of positivism or the 'other purposes and forms' of theological discourse." [1]

Falsification Principle

It was Karl Popper [2] who pointed out that the real test of a scientific theory is not its verifiability but its falsifiability. Whatever the theory may be, some verification will probably be forthcoming if one searches for it with sufficient diligence. The true scientist looks rather for what will falsify his theory. Irrefutability is not a strength but a weakness in the case of any belief. For if no state of affairs counts against that belief or could be imagined as counting against it, then the belief must be almost entirely vacuous. Popper was specially critical of the Freudian theory of the

[1] *The New Dialogue between Philosophy and Theology* (New York, 1966), pp. 66-67.
[2] *The Logic of Scientific Discovery* (London, 1960).

human psyche and the Marxist theory of history as illustrations of pseudo-scientific theories which suffer from the vice of irrefutability. Whatever happens, these theories find some way of accommodating it. Nothing that could possibly happen would be taken as counting against the theory. This simply shows the amorphous and vacuous character of such theories. A belief that is compatible with everything is like an amoeba that changes its shape continually as it ingests one particle of food after another. It is obvious that this criticism can easily be extended to Christian beliefs. Is the assertion "God is love" compatible with any and every state of affairs—with the Lisbon earthquake, with Auschwitz, with Hiroshima, with Biafra? Could you imagine anything that might happen which would force you to say "God is *not* love!" And if you cannot imagine anything of the sort, then does your assertion that God is love mean anything at all? If it is compatible with any and every state of affairs, is it not a vacuous statement?

The "love of God" is a rather notorious example of an expression which, at the hands of the theologian, may, in Anthony Flew's words, suffer "the death of a thousand qualifications". An idea gets so blurred, broadened and generalized that it really ceases to mean anything at all, and sentences which contain it have been reduced to vacuous statements. This particular abuse of language seems to constitute a special danger at present to ecumenical theologians. They want to be so inclusive in their use of terms that they end up by reducing these terms to mere ciphers that can no longer be usefully employed in intelligent discussion. An example of this blurring of terms is found in Hans Küng's recent book *The Church*. Expressions like "apostolic succession" and "infallibility" become so broad and generalized as to stultify rather than help ecumenical discussion. To say that the whole Church is successor to the apostles is to say something so obvious as to be meaningless, and does not help us to understand, e.g., the significance of the election of Matthias, Paul's claim to be an apostle, his remarks on apostolic gifts, or the problem of orders today. To swallow up infallibility in indefectibility is to evade

problems that must be considered honestly and sincerely if ecumenical progress is to be made. Where everything can mean anything, it usually means nothing.

II
NEW DEVELOPMENTS IN ANALYTICAL PHILOSOPHY

The basic challenges thrown down by the logical analysts
remain, and they call for care on the part of the theologian that
his language be as clear and coherent as possible, and that he
resist the temptation to seek shelter in obscurity, ambiguity and
vague but vacuous generalizations. But developments in analytical philosophy itself have presented the theologian with oppor-
tunities to work out the logic of religious language. Let me mention what some of these developments have been.

Principle of Use of Language

The first point has been the gradual erosion of the verification
principle, the very cornerstone of positivism. This principle has
run up against two difficulties. One is the difficulty of finding a
satisfactory formulation. In the case of a simple proposition like
"There is a cat on the mat", the question of empirical verification
is also simple—you go and look. "Napoleon was defeated at
Waterloo" presents rather more difficulty; no one can go and
look, but it is possible to predict that the assertion, if true, should
yield certain experiences if you look up old records. A general
scientific law presents further problems. To see what some of the
problems for the positivist were, one may compare the first edition of Alfred Ayer's *Language, Truth and Logic* with the
second edition in which he tries to reformulate the verification
principle. There are "strong" and "weak" forms of verification,
but in spite of all the attempts that have been made to reach an
adequate statement of the principle, I think one must agree with
a recent observation by Donald Hudson who says: "I do not
think that, in fact, a formulation of their verification principle,

entirely satisfactory to logical positivists, has ever been found." [3]
The other difficulty has been to establish the status of the verification principle as itself a meaningful proposition. It does not
seem to be self-evident, or a tautology like the first principles of
mathematics and logic. Yet it is not itself a verifiable proposition.
What is it then? John Wisdom was surely correct when he wrote:
"The fact is, the verification principle is a metaphysical proposition—a 'smashing' one, if I may be permitted the expression." [4]

The verification principle has for all intents and purposes been
succeeded by the principle of use. The meaning of any language
is to be found in the way it gets used. This creates a new situation for the analyst of religious language. He could never have
shown that such language is capable of empirical verification, for
it is a different kind of language from that of empirical discourse.
But the admission of the principle of use implies that because
religious language is different, it is not therefore nonsense and is
perhaps not merely an emotive language. But it is up to the theologian or the philosopher of religion to show what the use is, and
how important it is that we should use such a language.

Multiplicity of Kinds of Language

A second development, closely following on the first, has been
the recognition that there is a great multiplicity of kinds of language. There are many uses of language, and consequently there
are many languages. It was Ludwig Wittgenstein who coined the
expression "language games". The suggestion is that each type of
language has its own rules—i.e., its own logic—just as every
game has its own rules. Clearly, in fact, there is an internal logic
of religious language, a set of rules governing the way in which
this kind of talk may be used, and we immediately recognize at
least the grosser breaches of these rules. For instance, it makes
sense according to the rules of the religious language-game to say
"God is love", but it is a breach of the rules and nonsense to say

---

[3] *Ludwig Wittgenstein: The Bearing of His Philosophy on Religious
Belief* (London, 1968), pp. 20-21.
[4] *Philosophy and Psychoanalysis* (Oxford, 1953), p. 245.

"God weighs five billion tons". This is a category mistake in this particular logic. (I suspect that "God is dead" is equally a category mistake.) However, in the long run, one cannot remain content with an internal logic. One must also ask whether this particular game is worth playing, and whether and how it is related to other language games. The analyst may argue that even if religious language has its own internal logic, nevertheless this language does not cohere in the family of meaningful languages. On the other hand, William Hordern has argued that among all the language games that are played, religious language represents the Olympic Games—the games where the most ultimate and costly issues are decided.[5]

Wittgenstein also spoke of languages as "forms of life", and about this I shall have more to say later. In any case, the point is that the users of all kinds of languages are invited to say what the logic of each one is, and this is certainly a more empirical procedure than obtained in those theories which tried to lay down in advance what languages are to be regarded as meaningful, and what languages are to be regarded as nonsense.

"Analogue Models" of Language

Important also for the problem of religious language is the new interest in the oblique uses of language. The older analysts adhered to the so-called "picture theory" of language. We find it, for instance, in Bertrand Russell and in the early writings of Wittgenstein. In this view, the world is made up of an indefinite number of facts; corresponding to each fact is a proposition, such that the structure of the proposition copies or pictures the structure of the fact. No doubt this remains a plausible theory for simple propositions such as: "The cat sits on the mat." But the picture theory of language has now been generally abandoned.

One factor leading to the abandonment of the picture theory has been the course of development in physics. The language of physics was long taken as the paradigm of empirical language—indeed, there was even at one time a theory called

[5] *Speaking of God* (New York, 1964).

"physicalism", advocated by Rudolf Carnap and others. On this theory, all meaningful language is, in principle, reducible to the language of physics. However, the language of physics has become increasingly mysterious. It is now recognized that the atom and its constitutent particles cannot be "pictured" at all. We do in fact use a variety of models to elucidate atomic and sub-atomic phenomena, but these are non-picturing models, and we may even find it necessary to use a plurality of models not easily harmonized among themselves. These models of the contemporary physicist are not picture models but, as Max Black has called them, "analogue models". Ian Ramsey prefers to call them "disclosure models"—they do not literally picture the atom (or whatever it may be) but they do in some manner open it to our understanding.

In recognizing that there can be a use of language which does not picture but which nevertheless discloses in an indirect way, the contemporary logical analyst has once more broadened his view of language, and this time in a way that is very relevant to the problems of religious language. For believers have long recognized that their language is not a direct, literal, picturing language, but a language of symbols and analogues. Of course, it would be quite wrong to suppose that the symbols and analogues of religion function in the same way as those of physics. The electron, after all, though we cannot picture it, is still a physical entity. God-language is fundamentally different from electron-language. But the new interest in developing a logic of "analogue models" is bound to have implications of importance for a logic of religious language.

It is noteworthy, too, that some logical analysts who have discussed the claims of religion have themselves introduced into the discussion some very suggestive parables. One of the best known is John Wisdom's parable of the two men who argue as to whether or not a gardener comes to look after a plot of ground, and the kind of arguments which each adduces to support his point of view. This parable throws light on the nature of the controversy between theist and atheist, and seems to indicate that it comes finally to the tracing of different patterns in the world and in experience.[6] Basil Mitchell made telling use of the parable of the resistance fighter who meets a stranger, claiming to be head of the resistance movement, and the fighter is so impressed by his meeting with the stranger that he pledges unqualified obedience, in spite of all the ambiguities of the situation. This parable does help us to understand what "faith in God" means in an ambiguous world.[7] The examples themselves do not matter. What is important is that the logical analyst is willing to utilize this kind of oblique language to talk of the concerns of faith.

"Self-Ascriptive" Language

I turn next to the attention that is being paid to what is called "self-ascriptive" language. I have already alluded to the old doctrine of physicalism, according to which all meaningful language is, in principle, reducible to the language of physics. In such a view, human conduct itself would be considered in terms of a behavioristic psychology, which could in turn be translated into the language of physiology and ultimately into a purely physical language. Even if one does not go so far as physicalism, an empirical approach does seek to eliminate anything that is not open to observation by the senses. In particular, there is distrust of words like "mind", "spirit", "consciousness", and anything that savors of inner states or introspection. The empiricist is concerned with overt, observable facts. Thus, in order to bring human behavior within the scope of science, he must rigorously exclude everything that is not amenable to scientific observation —though some people will believe that such a procedure excludes precisely what is most distinctively human and personal.

However, recent developments in analytical philosophy do not favor the reductionist approach in the study of human behavior.

[6] See *Philosophy and Psychoanalysis,* pp. 149-68.
[7] *New Essays in Philosophical Theology,* ed. A. Flew and A. MacIntyre (London, 1955), pp. 103-05.

An important book which has upheld the independence and irreducibility of what we might call a "logic of persons" is Peter Strawson's *Individuals*. Consider such a verb as, let us say, "to love". When we use this verb in the third person, "he loves", then presumably it does describe an observable pattern of behavior which can be described in empirical terms. We may say that John loves his sister because we have observed his loving behavior. But when we use the verb in the first person, "I love", the case is different. I do not say I love my sister because I have observed my own behavior toward her over a period of time; rather, I am expressing an attitude which I know at first hand as a conscious (and, in this case, loving) agent. Are we to say then that the verb "to love" changes its meaning as it is conjugated, having one sense in its self-ascriptive use (first person) and another sense in its other-ascriptive use (third person)? This would be absurd. The truth surely is that a verb such as "to love" unites in a single meaning both an inner and an outer reference, and that it would be severely mutilated in its logic if we tried to reduce one side of the meaning to the other. In Strawson's words, "It is essential to the single kind of meaning which [such verbs] have that both ways of ascribing them should be perfectly in order." [8]

Strawson develops another argument which has to do with the structure of ordinary language. There are, he contends, two basic or primitive logics, and practically everyone "sees the world" in terms of these. Everyone knows that whereas it makes sense to say, "John weighs one hundred and forty pounds and the table weighs eighty pounds," it does not make sense to say, "John is intelligent and the table is stupid." There are, in fact, built into the language, appropriate ways of talking about things and appropriate ways of talking about persons, and the second type of talk cannot be collapsed into the first. Of course, one might argue that our language is mistaken in this. Strawson is simply describing what is in fact the state of affairs—that we do distin-

---

[8] *Individuals: An Essay in Descriptive Metaphysics* (Garden City, 1963), pp. 106-07.

guish the two great categories of persons and things and have a distinct logic for each.

The relevance of these investigations to the problem of religious language is obvious. Religious language is very much a language of persons. It would assuredly be destroyed if the language of persons were reduced to the level of the impersonal. The further exploration of the meaning and logic of persons, opened up for us by secular philosophy, is a problem which the theologian and philosopher of religion must not neglect.

Language as a "Form of Life"

Of great importance is the contemporary emphasis on setting language in its human context. The earlier style of logic analysis might, with considerable justice, have been accused of a certain distorting kind of abstraction. Language was considered as words and sentences, to be scrutinized almost in a vacuum in terms of logic and syntax. But, in fact, language is the transcript of living speech among human beings. Language is always someone's language, and it is always addressed to someone. The home of language is the human community in which it is spoken and heard. The question of its meaning or lack of meaning can be decided only by seeing it as a channel of communication among persons.

In discussing both the need to put language in its human context and the earlier point about the nature of self-ascriptive language, it has become apparent that in the recent developments of analytical philosophy, there is emerging something like a convergence upon some of the interests of existentialist philosophy. It is recognized that logical analysis must be related to existential analysis, for language is itself a basic existential characteristic. Existentialism and empiricism are perhaps the two great secular philosophies of our time, but in their respective investigations into the phenomenon of language they seem to be finding some common ground. In particular, it is not difficult to find parallels between the treatment of language in the philosophy of Heidegger and some of the reflections of the later Wittgenstein.

Possibility of Descriptive Metaphysics

I pass finally to what is the most surprising development of all, though I do not think that it is any more important than those which we have already considered. This last point concerns the renewed interest among logical analysts in the possibility of metaphysics. In the iconoclastic days of logical positivism, metaphysics was dismissed, along with ethics and theology, as mere pseudo-philosophy. As the polemical phase passed, attempts were made first to rehabilitate ethics and to argue that ethical language has some rational basis and is not just evincing emotion. The rescue operations were extended to religion, though in accounts of the matter, such as that of Richard Braithwaite, an attempt was made to assimilate religious belief to moral belief and to avoid an interpretation that would lead into methaphysics. These efforts to rehabilitate ethics and religion could be regarded as pragmatic. After all, morality and religion are facts of life, and some account of them must be offered. But until very recently the logical analyst would not allow that any metaphysical discussion of these matters is possible—and this view is still widely held.

A straw in the wind was the book *Metaphysical Beliefs*,[9] edited by Alastair MacIntyre and published as long ago as 1957. While the writers of this book agreed that "traditional metaphysics are dead", they were convinced that there are issues in metaphysics that need to be revived and studied anew. A further important step toward grappling anew with the problem of metaphysics came with the distinction made by Peter Strawson (in the book quoted above) between what he called "descriptive" metaphysics and "revisionary" metaphysics. Strawson gave his approval to the former of these enterprises. Descriptive metaphysics sets out to tell us what are the most general categories under which men organize their experience, and proceeds to analyze these categories. Revisionary metaphysics, according to Strawson, is a more dubious undertaking. This second kind of metaphysics tells us

[9] *Metaphysical Beliefs*, ed. A. MacIntyre (London, 1957).

what *ought to be* the way in which we understand our experience. Kant's critical philosophy would, roughly speaking, be an example of a descriptive metaphysic, while the system of Hegel would illustrate revisionary metaphysics.

However, the distinction between the two types of metaphysics is not an easy one to maintain. At what point does description end and pass over into interpretation? Can there be a descriptive metaphysic which is not also an interpretative metaphysic? Then we would have to ask at what point an interpretative metaphysic passes over into a revisionary metaphysic.

Perhaps the most impressive essay on metaphysics by an analytical philosopher is the book *The Mystery of Existence* by Milton K. Munitz.[10] Munitz takes up a metaphysical question, and a very famous one it is: "Why is there a world?" or, in the formulation of Leibnitz, "Why is there anything at all, rather than just nothing?" On the other hand, Munitz defends this question against the positivists who would dismiss it as meaningless. He argues that it can be formulated in such a way that it is a real question. On the other hand, he argues also that there is no rational way of answering this question, and here his criticisms seem to be directed chiefly against the traditional natural theology. Outstanding features of the book include the analysis which Munitz offers of the logical status of the word "world", and his careful inquiry into the various kinds of metaphysics that have been practiced in the course of the history of philosophy.

The analytical interest in metaphysics is still in its early stages, but it promises to be exciting. It may be that the metaphysical enterprise can be made to get moving again, though it will have absorbed enough of analytical stringency and honesty to be saved from some of those excesses of speculation that have tended to discredit metaphysics in the past. The relevance of this new development for theology and the philosophy of religion is too obvious to call for any comment.

In this article I have directed attention to the work of secular

[10] *The Mystery of Existence: An Essay in Philosophical Cosmology* (New York, 1965).

philosophers whose interest in theology, if they have any at all, is at most tangential. Nevertheless, I have tried to show that the work they are doing is full of interest to the theologian. At the very least, it can save him from loose and misleading ways of using language. But, more than this, it surely opens up fruitful ways in which the work of theology can be done in the contemporary world. Many theologians have already learned from the analytic philosophers and are applying their insights. Chief among them is Ian T. Ramsey, now the learned bishop of Durham. Others are Frederick Ferré, John Hick, Dallas High and many others in England and the United States. Many interesting developments can be expected from this meeting of philosophy and theology.

PART III
DOCUMENTATION
CONCILIUM

Office of the Executive Secretary
Nijmegen, Netherlands

Concilium General Secretariat/*Nijmegen, Netherlands*

A Note on the Work
of Henry Duméry

One of the classic debates in fundamental theology revolves around the question whether this fundamental theology is genuine theology or philosophy. An author who put this whole problem in an entirely new light is the somewhat solitary figure of Henry Duméry. We do not know whether this isolation came about because his works were condemned by Rome,[1] or because he deals with a speculative problem which at first sight does not look particularly interesting at present, or because since Barth we approach the opposition between reason and faith, philosophy and theology, differently today, or because since the advent of phenomenology we have become wary of any return to metaphysics.

[1] On June 4, 1958, the following works of Duméry, then 38 years old, were condemned: *Philosophie de la religion* (2 vols.) (Paris, 1957); *Critique et religion* (Paris, 1957); *Le problème de Dieu en philosophie de la religion* (Bruges, 1957); *La Foi n'est pas un cri* (Tournai, 1957); cf. *A.A.S.* 51 (1958), p. 432. After having requested and obtained laicization in the normal way, Duméry continued to work on the same lines. This has produced some studies of Blondel and a book about God. Although his *Traité sur Dieu* is as good as finished, it will still take some time before it will appear, according to information given us by S. Breton. For a brief survey of Duméry's main points, I refer to J. Lacroix, "La philosophie de la religion d'Henry Duméry," in *Panorama de la Philosophie française contemporaine* (Paris, 1966), pp. 84-90; for a more detailed and personal introduction, see H. van Luijk, *Philosophie du fait chrétien* (Paris/Bruges, 1964), with an extensive bibliography.

Although all these aspects are worthy of interest, lack of space forces us to concentrate on what is most typical of Duméry's work—namely, his search for a method which allows us to judge the act of faith and the themes of this faith by their validity. Here he has made use of Husserl's phenomenology and Blondel's integral justification of faith. For his *method* Duméry tries to arrive at this critical judgment by looking at it from outside the faith.[2] This seems to be the most characteristic feature of his method. It is at the same time the most vulnerable spot which exposes him constantly to attacks from believers, whether theologians or not.[3] The difficulties can be brought together under two main questions: 1. How can the non-believer (methodologically speaking) make a valid judgment about faith? 2. Is the theological justification of the faith not scientific enough?

To the last question, Duméry would say that, in spite of his scientific method, the theologian moves within the self-evidence of faith. If the theologian wants to pass from the "native" attitude (believing and practicing theology) to the "critical" attitude, he must follow a method which suspends the act of faith and the analysis of its content, and so apply what Husserl called "epoché". From this angle one can then come to a rational judgment about the general validity of belief. It is then possible, also in the eyes of the non-believer, to strip the faith of its character of something that is pre-judged. This makes it also possible to clear up the misunderstanding with regard to Duméry: how can the non-believer (in the methodological sense) judge, in a way which is valid for both believer and non-believer, about the act

---

[2] "We are looking for a method which would enable the philosopher to investigate the condition of a religious man and to decide what is and what is not rationally valid there" (*Critique et Religion*, p. 45); "This critical investigation compels the conscience to detach itself from any belief as an immediate commitment" (*ibid.*, p. 24).

[3] This methodological detachment from faith has been understood by many as a rejection of the faith as a primitive phase, unworthy of man. Nothing is more alien to Duméry's thought: "I treat of faith as a specific object, which cannot be reduced to anything else. The aim of a critical approach is not to explain away, but to understand. To understand is not to explain—that is, it does not break something down into quantitative elements (*Philosophie de la Religion* I, p. ix).

of faith, the expression of it in a creed and reflection upon it in theology? The believer can obviously justify himself by appealing to revelation, but if he is conscious of his belief he cannot escape the fact that the act of faith also includes *generally* valid processes, and the believer as well as Scripture itself expresses the content of the faith within the logic of a human language.

Linguistic analysis and hermeneutics today are busily occupied with this aspect. The generally valid processes which operate in the act of faith are, in a limited way, illumined by Freudian psychology and the "human" sciences that arose from it. Duméry wants to throw light on the limitation of this psychological approach (e.g., faith is a projection, or faith is an illusion) in a way which also validates these processes by a critical method that can break through the hermeneutical circles of the traditional theological analysis of faith. For this purpose he develops a method which must be tested as a method, and judged by its rational merit.

There is, of course, no point in meeting this formidable attempt undertaken by Duméry with the simple observation that this reduces faith to a purely subjective affair. What this new kind of religious philosopher has pointed to as the two most urgent problems for modern man, faced with an existing faith, and the speculative power embodied in his work,[4] will remain of permanent value.[5] The first of these two problems, the search for the *logos* in the institutionalized and active expression of the

[4] On consulting S. Breton about this documentation which was originally intended to be far more detailed but had to be reduced for lack of space, our friend wrote: "I am particularly astonished that at a time when theologians indulge in an unprecedented freedom of doctrinal discussion, where there is so little structural thought and the real problems are so rarely faced, so little is said about such work as has been done by Duméry. . . . Unless one is content with some descriptive phenomenologies or some morphology of the sacred, any understanding in depth must be tested by some philosophy, at whatever risk. What is important is that such a philosophy can put forward real problems and, if necessary, shake people out of a long-standing torpor."

[5] L. Boros, "Entschematisiertes Christentum?" in *Orientierung* 22 (1958), pp. 152-54 and 168-72; H. Duméry, "Foi, raison et sympathie," in *L'Aventure de l'esprit* II (Paris, 1964), pp. 129-43; "Philosophie et religion," in *Bulletin de la Soc. franç. de Phil.* 59 (April-June, 1965),

faith, has already witnessed a great scientific advance in herme-neutics and the methods of linguistic analysis. The second, more speculative and reaching beyond phenomenology, the search for the general valid rationality which lies behind the phenomenon of belief, has so far been tackled mainly by French students.[6]

We thought that this work of Duméry should at least be men-tioned in a volume where various attempts are discussed to lead contemporary fundamental theology out of its present impasse. Here a philosophy of religion, which is deliberately also an anthropology, has put before us problems which we cannot ne-glect with impunity.

---

p. 2; L. Dupré, "The Problem of a Philosophy of Christianity," in *The Modern Schoolman* 44 (1966), pp. 161-68.

[6] R. Virgoulay, "Foi et critique. La philosophie de la religion et la théologie," in *Rech. de Sc. Rel.* 54 (1966), pp. 497-529; J. Mansir, "Reflexions sur les conditions d'une critique philosophique de la foi," in *Rev. des Sc. Phil. et Théol.* 51 (1967), pp. 149-85; A. Thiry, "Philosophie du fait chrétien," in *N. R. Th.* 88 (1966), pp. 693-97; G. van Riet, "Idéalisme et christianisme," in *Rev. de Phil. de Louvain* 56 (1958), pp. 316-428; "Philosophie de la religion et théologie," *ibid.* 57 (1959), pp. 415-37; J. Mouroux, "La tentative de H. Duméry," in *Rev. des Sc. Phil. et Théol.* 43 (1959), pp. 95-102; J. Mouroux and H. Duméry, "Postface à une dialogue," *ibid.* 44 (1960), pp. 89-97; L. Morren, "La fonction religieuse de la raison," in *N. R. Th.* 90 (Jan. 1968), pp. 23-30; R. Marlé, "La philosophie de la religion de H. Duméry," in *Rev. Sc. Rel.* 47 (1959), pp. 225-41; L. Malevez, "Le fait Jésus et la conscience projective dans l'oeuvre de H. Duméry," in *N. R. Th.* 89 (1967), pp. 417-20.

BIOGRAPHICAL NOTES

CLAUDE GEFFRÉ, O.P.: Born in France in 1926, he was ordained in 1953. He studied at St. Sulpice in Paris, at the Angelicum in Rome, and at the Saulchoir, where he is now professor of dogmatic theology. He is a frequent contributor to *Revue des Sciences philosophiques et théologiques* and *La Vie Spirituelle*.

RENÉ LATOURELLE, S.J.: Born in Montreal in 1918, he was ordained in 1950. He studied at the University of Montreal and at the Gregorian in Rome. He received an M.A. in French literature, a licentiate in philosophy, and doctorates in history and theology. He has been professor of fundamental theology at the Gregorian since 1959. His published works include *Theologia, scientia sacra* (Rome, 1965) and *Theology of Revelation* (New York, 1968).

RAYMOND PANIKKAR: Born in Barcelona in 1918, he was ordained in 1946. He studied at the universities of Bonn, Barcelona and Madrid, and also in Rome. He received a licentiate in chemistry and doctorates in philosophy, science and theology. He is Senior Research Fellow at the Institute for Advanced Studies in Philosophy at Banaras Hindu University in India, and Visiting Professor of the Center for the Study of World Religions at Harvard Divinity School. His publications include *The Unknown Christ of Hinduism* (London, 1964) and *Offenbarung und Verkündigung, Indische Briefe* (Freiburg, 1967).

HEINRICH FRIES: Born in Germany in 1911, he was ordained in 1936. He studied at the University of Tubingen, receiving his doctorate in theology. He is a professor of fundamental theology and a director of the Institute of Ecumenical Theology in Munich. His published works include *Herausgeforderter Glaube* (Munich, 1968). He is editor of the two-volume work *Handbuch Theologischer Grundbegriffe* (Munich, 1962), for which he authored articles on unity, God, the Church, religion, signs and miracles.

JUAN SEGUNDO, S.J.: Born in Uruguay in 1925, he was ordained in 1955. He studied at St. Albert in Louvain and at the University of Paris, receiving a licentiate in theology and a doctorate in literature. Director of the Centro Pedro Fabro, a center of sociological investigation and action,

179

his published works include *Berdiaeff. Une conception chrétienne de la Personne* (Paris, 1963) and the two-volume *La Cristiandad, una utopía* (Montevideo, 1963).

JAN WALGRAVE, O.P.: Born in Belgium in 1911, he was ordained in 1935. He studied at the University of Louvain, receiving his doctorate in theology. He is professor of fundamental theology at the Centrum voor kerkelijke in Louvain. His published works include *Op de grondslag van het woord* (Louvain, 1965) and *Geloof en theologie in de crisis* (Tielt, 1968).

JOSEPH CAHILL, S.J.: Born in Chicago in 1923, he was ordained in 1956. Possessing a doctorate in theology, he teaches at the University of Notre Dame, Indiana. His published works include *Eschatological Occurrence* (1960) and *A Dictionary of Biblical Theology* (1967).

KARL RAHNER, S.J.: Born in Freiburg im Breisgau in 1904, he was ordained in 1932. He studied at Freiburg im Breisgau and at Innsbruck in Austria, receiving his doctorate in theology. He has been professor of dogmatic theology and of the history of dogma at the University of Münster since 1967. His many and important publications include *Theology of Pastoral Action* (London, 1968), *Servants of the Lord* (London, 1968) and *The Christian of the Future* (London, 1966).

LANGDON GILKEY: Born in Chicago in 1919, he is a member of the Reformed Church. He studied at the universities of Harvard and Columbia and at the Union Theological Seminary. He received his doctorate in philosophy, and has been a professor in the Divinity School of Chicago University since 1963. His publications include *The Renewal of God-Language* (1968).

JOHN MACQUARRIE: Born in Scotland in 1919, he was ordained in the Anglican Church in 1965. He received doctorates in philosophy, literature and theology, and has been professor of systematic theology at the Union Theological Seminary of New York since 1962. His publications include *Principles of Christian Theology* (London, 1966) and *God-Talk. An Examination of the Language and Logic of Theology* (London, 1967).

International Publishers of CONCILIUM

ENGLISH EDITION
Paulist Press
Paramus, N.J., U.S.A.

Burns & Oates Ltd.
25 Ashley Place
London, S.W.1

DUTCH EDITION
Uitgeverij Paul Brand, N.V.
Hilversum, Netherlands

FRENCH EDITION
Maison Mame
Tours/Paris, France

JAPANESE EDITION (PARTIAL)
Nansôsha
Tokyo, Japan

GERMAN EDITION
Verlagsanstalt Benziger & Co., A.G.
Einsiedeln, Switzerland

Matthias Grunewald-Verlag
Mainz, W. Germany

SPANISH EDITION
Ediciones Guadarrama
Madrid, Spain

PORTUGUESE EDITION
Livraria Morais Editora, Ltda.
Lisbon, Portugal

ITALIAN EDITION
Editrice Queriniana
Brescia, Italy

POLISH EDITION (PARTIAL)
Pallottinum
Poznan-Warsaw, Poland